EXECUTIVE OFFICE OF THE PRESIDENT
OFFICE OF MANAGEMENT AND BUDGET
WASHINGTON, D.C. 20503

July 14, 2015

The Honorable John A. Boehner
Speaker of the House of Representatives
Washington, D.C. 20510

Dear Mr. Speaker:

    Section 1106 of Title 31, United States Code, requests that the President send to the Congress a supplemental update of the Budget that was transmitted to the Congress earlier in the year. This enclosed supplemental update of the Budget, commonly known as the Mid-Session Review, contains revised estimates of receipts, outlays, budget authority, and the budget deficit for fiscal years 2015 through 2025.

Sincerely,

Shaun Donovan
Director

Enclosure

Identical Letter Sent to The President of the Senate

# TABLE OF CONTENTS

*Page*

List of Tables ................................................................................................................... iii

Summary ............................................................................................................................ 1

Economic Assumptions ..................................................................................................... 5

Receipts ............................................................................................................................ 11

Expenditures ................................................................................................................... 15

Summary Tables ............................................................................................................. 21

## GENERAL NOTES

1. Unless otherwise noted, years referenced for budget data are fiscal years, and years referenced for economic data are calendar years.

2. All totals in the text and tables include both on-budget and off-budget spending and receipts unless otherwise noted.

3. Details in the tables and text may not add to totals due to rounding.

4. Web address: *http://www.budget.gov*

# LIST OF TABLES

| | | Page |
|---|---|---|
| Table 1. | Changes in Deficits from the February Budget | 4 |
| Table 2. | Economic Assumptions | 6 |
| Table 3. | Comparison of Economic Assumptions | 8 |
| Table 4. | Change in Receipts | 13 |
| Table 5. | Change in Outlays | 19 |
| Table S–1. | Budget Totals | 23 |
| Table S–2. | Effect of Budget Proposals on Projected Deficits | 24 |
| Table S–3. | Cumulative Deficit Reduction | 26 |
| Table S–4. | Adjusted Baseline by Category | 28 |
| Table S–5. | Proposed Budget by Category | 30 |
| Table S–6. | Proposed Budget by Category as a Percent of GDP | 32 |
| Table S–7. | Bridge from Balanced Budget and Emergency Deficit Control Act (BBEDCA) Baseline to Adjusted Baseline | 34 |
| Table S–8. | Mandatory and Receipt Proposals | 35 |
| Table S–9. | Funding Levels for Appropriated ("Discretionary") Programs by Category | 60 |
| Table S–10. | Funding Levels for Appropriated ("Discretionary") Programs by Agency | 62 |
| Table S–11. | Federal Government Financing and Debt | 64 |

# SUMMARY

This Mid-Session Review (MSR) updates the Administration's estimates for outlays, receipts, and the deficit for economic, legislative, and other changes that have occurred since the President's 2016 Budget (Budget) was released in February. The 2015 deficit is now projected to be $455 billion, $128 billion lower than the $583 billion deficit projected in February. As a percentage of gross domestic product (GDP), the 2015 deficit is now projected to equal 2.6 percent, down from 2.8 percent of GDP last year and down from the 3.2 percent projected in February. Going forward, the MSR estimates that the deficit will fall to between 2.2 and 2.4 percent of GDP for 2016 through 2018 and stabilize at 2.7 percent of GDP in the second half of the 10-year budget window. The MSR also confirms that the Budget's policies meet the key test of fiscal sustainability by stabilizing Federal debt as a share of the economy. The Budget achieves that goal while also investing in growth and opportunity for all.

## CONTINUING ECONOMIC GROWTH AND PROGRESS

Since taking office, the President has fought to strengthen the economy and expand opportunity for middle-class families. The President's decisive actions during the financial crisis brought the economy back from the brink, paving the way for the increasingly strong growth seen today. The Administration pushed the Recovery Act to jumpstart the economy and create jobs; rescued the auto industry from near collapse; secured the Dodd-Frank Wall Street Reform legislation to help prevent future financial crises; and fought for passage of the Affordable Care Act to provide insurance coverage to millions of Americans and help slow the growth of health care costs.

Today, the American people's determination and resilience, coupled with the Administration's efforts, are driving the economy full steam ahead. Businesses have added 12.8 million jobs over 64 straight months of private-sector job growth. Since the beginning of 2014, job growth has accelerated and the unemployment rate has fallen 1.4 percent to 5.3 percent. The United States is producing more oil than it imports, and domestic natural gas and wind production has been setting record highs. After five years of implementation of the Affordable Care Act, more than 16 million people have gained health insurance coverage, bringing the uninsured rate to the lowest level on record. Meanwhile, health care prices have grown at the slowest rate in nearly 50 years during the period since the Affordable Care Act became law.

This represents significant progress, but more can be done to accelerate growth and expand opportunity for all Americans. The MSR shows how we can invest in America's future and commit ourselves to an economy that rewards hard work, generates rising incomes, and allows everyone to share in the prosperity of a growing America, while also finishing the task of putting the Nation on a sustainable fiscal path.

## STRENGTHENING THE NATION'S FISCAL OUTLOOK

Under the President's leadership, the deficit has already been cut by more than two thirds as a share of the economy, representing the most rapid sustained deficit reduction since World War II. The medium-term and long-term budget outlook have also improved substantially over the last five years.

To further strengthen America's long-term fiscal outlook and the economy and set the Nation on a sustainable fiscal path, the Budget proposes $1.75 trillion of deficit reduction over 10 years, primarily from health, tax, and immigration reforms. It includes about $370 billion of health savings that grow over time, extending the life of the Medicare Trust Fund and building on the Affordable Care Act with further incentives to improve quality and control health care cost growth. It obtains about $640 billion in deficit reduction from reducing tax benefits for high-income households. It also reflects the President's support for pro-growth, common-sense immigration reform, which the Congressional Budget Office estimates would reduce the deficit by about $170 billion over 10 years and by almost $1 trillion over two decades, and the Social Security Administration estimates would reduce Social Security's 75-year shortfall by 8 percent.

The policies in the Budget show that investments in growth and opportunity are also compatible with putting the Nation's finances on a strong and sustainable path. The MSR shows that, under the Budget's policies, deficits decline to a low of 2.2 percent of GDP before stabilizing at 2.7 percent of GDP in the later years of the budget window, with the debt holding stable as a share of GDP starting in 2018.

## INVESTING IN AMERICA'S FUTURE

America's promise has always been that if we work hard, we can change our circumstances for the better. The economy cannot truly succeed until we live up to that promise. The Budget lays out a strategy to reach that promise, by investing in the drivers of growth and opportunity for all Americans.

Because we cannot afford a return to mindless austerity, the Budget reverses the harmful spending cuts known as sequestration and makes needed investments in key priorities that are more than paid for with smart spending cuts, program integrity measures, and common-sense tax loophole closers. The Bipartisan Budget Act of 2013 reversed a portion of sequestration and allowed for higher investment levels in 2014 and 2015, but it did nothing to alleviate sequestration in 2016. In the absence of congressional action, both non-defense and base defense discretionary funding in 2016 will be at the lowest level in a decade, adjusted for inflation.

The Budget's paid-for increases in discretionary funding make room for a range of domestic and security investments that will help move the Nation forward. These include investments to strengthen the economy by improving the education and skills of the U.S. workforce, accelerating scientific discovery, and continuing to bolster manufacturing. The Budget also proposes to further accelerate growth and opportunity and create jobs through pro-work, pro-family tax reforms and through mandatory investments—in surface transportation infrastructure, universal pre-kindergarten, child care assistance for middle-class and working families, and other initiatives.

To ensure America remains a magnet for jobs, the Budget builds on investments in manufacturing and innovation—including through clean energy technology programs and tax policies that position America as a global clean energy leader with a strong and modern energy infrastructure. To fix the Nation's roads and bridges and create more middle class jobs, it continues the progress toward building a 21st-Century infrastructure. The Budget invests in education and job training to give all Americans the skills they need to compete in the global economy. It also provides resources to programs that help create opportunity and economic mobility for all, and it reforms the tax system to better support and reward work.

To further the progress made to prevent another financial crisis such as the one the Nation saw in 2008, the Budget supports the financial stability efforts launched through the Dodd-Frank Wall Street Reform and Consumer Protection Act. The Budget also invests in climate preparedness and resilience—providing necessary tools, technical assistance, and on-the-ground partnership to communities that are dealing with the effects of climate change today.

The Budget fully supports the President's Management Agenda, a comprehensive and forward-looking plan to modernize and improve government to ultimately deliver better, faster, and smarter services to citizens and businesses. It makes investments to drive forward progress on cross-agency management priorities, including funding to support the teams leading cross-agency priority goals and to promote Federal spending transparency. It also increases support for ongoing initiatives—such as the U.S. Digital Service, PortfolioStat, Freeze the Footprint, and Open Data—that have already had an impact on improving Government operations.

The Budget recognizes that while America is a world leader in domestic economic growth, it must also continue to promote U.S. national security interests while mobilizing the international community to address global challenges to the Nation's safety and security. That is why the Budget further advances national security priorities by proposing the funding increases needed to execute the President's defense strategy. The Budget supports America's continued fight to degrade and ultimately defeat the Islamic State of Iraq and the Levant. The Budget continues the transition in Afghanistan, while also supporting European reassurance efforts to counter Russia's aggressive actions. It advances security, prosperity, and economic growth in the Central America Region to address the root causes of migration, continues the progress made to reassert American leadership in the Asia-Pacific region, and strengthens U.S. global health security. The Budget also upholds the Nation's duty to care for its veterans who have risked their lives to serve America.

In contrast, Congressional Republicans' 2016 budget framework would lock in the mindless austerity of sequestration and weaken America's economy at a time of accelerating growth. Compared to the President's Budget, the cuts would result in tens of thousands of the Nation's most vulnerable children losing access to high quality early education and millions fewer workers receiving job training and employment services. By starving the Nation of investments that support long-term broadly shared growth, sequestration would hurt the economy, the middle class, and Americans working hard to reach the middle class.

Sequestration funding levels in the base budget combined with the inappropriate use of Overseas Contingency Operations (OCO) funds for base requirements would also put our national security at unnecessary risk. This approach fails to provide the stable, multi-year budget on which defense planning is based, undermines a mechanism meant to fund incremental costs of overseas conflicts, and locks in unacceptable funding cuts for national security activities at non-defense agencies such as State, USAID, and Homeland Security. More broadly, the strength of our economy and the security of our Nation are linked. That is why the President has been clear that he is not willing to lock in sequestration going forward, nor will he accept fixes to defense without also fixing non-defense.

The only path forward on the budget is a bipartisan, common-sense solution, one that reverses sequestration for defense and non-defense priorities, as Congress did on a bipartisan basis two years ago and as Members from both parties have urged. That is the approach that the President's 2016 Budget embodies.

## Table 1. CHANGES IN DEFICITS FROM THE FEBRUARY BUDGET
(In billions of dollars)

| | 2015 | 2016 | 2017 | 2018 | 2019 | 2020 | 2021 | 2022 | 2023 | 2024 | 2025 | 2016–2020 | 2016–2025 |
|---|---|---|---|---|---|---|---|---|---|---|---|---|---|
| 2016 Budget deficit | 583 | 474 | 463 | 479 | 518 | 554 | 600 | 626 | 635 | 639 | 687 | | |
| Percent of GDP | 3.2% | 2.5% | 2.3% | 2.3% | 2.4% | 2.5% | 2.6% | 2.6% | 2.5% | 2.4% | 2.5% | | |
| **Enacted legislation and policy changes:** | | | | | | | | | | | | | |
| Medicare Access and CHIP Reauthorization Act of 2015 | * | –1 | 4 | 2 | –2 | –1 | –* | * | 2 | 2 | 4 | 1 | 8 |
| Other enacted legislation[1] | –* | * | –* | –1 | –* | * | * | * | –* | –* | –* | –1 | –1 |
| **Proposals to reflect Military Compensation and Retirement Modernization Commission recommendations:** | | | | | | | | | | | | | |
| Scoreable effect | | * | * | * | * | * | * | * | * | * | * | 1 | 3 |
| Non-scoreable and discretionary effects | | * | * | 1 | 1 | 2 | 2 | 2 | 2 | 3 | 3 | 4 | 16 |
| Debt service | –* | –* | * | * | * | * | * | * | * | 1 | 1 | * | 3 |
| Subtotal, enacted legislation and policy changes | –* | –1 | 3 | 3 | –1 | 1 | 2 | 3 | 5 | 5 | 8 | 5 | 29 |
| **Economic and technical reestimates:** | | | | | | | | | | | | | |
| Receipts | –72 | –32 | 15 | 47 | 67 | 62 | 62 | 69 | 79 | 84 | 86 | 159 | 539 |
| **Outlays:** | | | | | | | | | | | | | |
| Discretionary programs | –23 | 1 | 5 | 6 | 4 | 2 | 2 | 1 | 1 | 1 | 1 | 18 | 23 |
| **Mandatory:** | | | | | | | | | | | | | |
| Social Security | –7 | –14 | –19 | –21 | –22 | –24 | –24 | –25 | –25 | –26 | –27 | –100 | –229 |
| Medicare | 7 | 1 | 9 | 12 | 9 | 10 | 10 | 11 | 13 | 11 | 12 | 41 | 97 |
| Premium tax credits and cost-sharing reductions | –3 | –* | 6 | 7 | 5 | 6 | 7 | 7 | 7 | 7 | 8 | 24 | 59 |
| Immigration reform | | –3 | –1 | –3 | –4 | –8 | –4 | –5 | –6 | –8 | –6 | –19 | –48 |
| Unemployment compensation | –4 | –3 | –3 | –4 | –4 | –4 | –4 | –4 | –5 | –5 | –5 | –18 | –41 |
| Medicaid | 14 | 30 | 5 | 2 | 3 | 2 | 1 | * | –1 | –1 | –1 | 41 | 39 |
| Veterans programs | –3 | –1 | –1 | –2 | –2 | –2 | –3 | –3 | –3 | –3 | –3 | –8 | –22 |
| Civilian and military retirement | 1 | 1 | 1 | 1 | 1 | 2 | 2 | 2 | 2 | 2 | 3 | 7 | 18 |
| Child Tax Credit | –1 | 1 | 1 | 1 | 2 | 2 | 2 | 2 | 2 | 2 | 2 | 7 | 17 |
| Supplemental Security Income | –1 | –1 | –1 | –1 | –2 | –2 | –2 | –2 | –2 | –2 | –2 | –7 | –16 |
| Other[2] | –17 | 10 | 10 | 14 | 8 | 4 | 2 | –5 | –* | 17 | 5 | 46 | 65 |
| Total mandatory | –13 | 20 | 7 | 6 | –5 | –15 | –13 | –22 | –17 | –5 | –15 | 13 | –60 |
| Net interest[3] | –19 | –33 | –56 | –59 | –50 | –41 | –36 | –33 | –31 | –28 | –25 | –239 | –393 |
| Subtotal, outlays | –56 | –12 | –45 | –47 | –51 | –54 | –48 | –54 | –48 | –33 | –39 | –208 | –430 |
| Subtotal, economic and technical reestimates | –128 | –44 | –30 | –* | 17 | 8 | 14 | 15 | 32 | 51 | 47 | –49 | 109 |
| Total, changes | –128 | –45 | –26 | 2 | 16 | 9 | 16 | 18 | 37 | 56 | 55 | –44 | 137 |
| Mid-Session Review deficit | 455 | 429 | 436 | 481 | 533 | 563 | 617 | 643 | 672 | 695 | 742 | | |
| Percent of GDP | 2.6% | 2.3% | 2.2% | 2.4% | 2.5% | 2.5% | 2.7% | 2.7% | 2.7% | 2.7% | 2.7% | | |

Note: positive figures represent higher outlays or lower receipts.

*$500 million or less.

[1] The Trade Preference Extension Act of 2015 (P.L. 114–27), which enacted a number of Administration proposals, including extensions of the African Growth and Opportunity Act, the Generalized System of Preferences, and Trade Adjustment Assistance, was enacted too late to be included in the MSR estimates.

[2] Includes change in allowance for future disaster costs.

[3] Includes debt service on all reestimates.

# ECONOMIC ASSUMPTIONS

This Mid-Session Review (MSR) updates the economic forecast from the 2016 Budget, which was finalized in November and released with the Budget in February. The Budget forecast projected a strengthening economic recovery, with growth staying above the long-term potential growth rate over the next several years. Unemployment was expected to decline as the economy recovered, and inflation was expected to remain below 2 percent in the near term before rising to a stable and moderate pace. Interest rates were expected to remain low in the near term, but to rise gradually in the medium term. The MSR forecast, completed on June 2, maintains this overall outlook with modifications to take account of a pause in economic growth early this year, the drop in the unemployment rate since the Budget economic forecast was finalized in November, the rapid drop in oil prices since November, a reassessment of projected interest rates, and other factors.

From the second quarter of 2009 through the first quarter of 2015, real GDP increased by a cumulative 13.5 percent. In early 2010, following the resumption of real GDP growth, the private sector began adding jobs. Since then, private-sector employment has increased steadily, 12.8 million new jobs have been created, and the unemployment rate has declined from its peak of 10.0 percent in October 2009 to 5.3 percent in June. Labor market progress has accelerated, with more private-sector jobs created in 2014 than in any year since 1997, and with continued strong job growth in the first half of 2015. The housing market has also begun to contribute to the recovery. The steep decline in residential investment ended in 2010, and housing activity is recovering at a gradual pace.

Administration policies contributed to the economic revival, as did automatic fiscal stabilizers such as Unemployment Insurance. The American Recovery and Reinvestment Act was passed soon after the President took office, at a time when the economy was losing nearly 800,000 jobs per month and after real GDP fell at an annual rate of 8.2 percent in the fourth quarter of 2008. The Administration's prompt action helped to reverse these precipitous declines and opened the way to a sustained economic recovery. Additional actions by the Administration and Congress, including the passage of the temporary payroll tax holiday as part of legislation enacted in December 2010, provided additional support to demand and fostered continued growth.

Although Administration actions helped spark the initial stages of the ongoing recovery, restrictive fiscal policies, including the across-the-board cuts imposed under sequestration in 2013, and a series of manufactured crises, including a Government shutdown in October 2013, held back GDP and job growth. The Bipartisan Budget Act of 2013 and the subsequent Consolidated Appropriations Act of 2014 reduced the economic uncertainty created by fiscal policy and partially reversed the sharp cuts imposed under sequestration. Federal spending was approximately neutral for GDP growth last year, and is expected to make a moderate contribution to GDP growth this year.

Although the fiscal constraint on the economy lessened, the economy was affected early this year by unusually cold and snowy weather and labor disputes at West Coast ports, which dampened economic activity in the first quarter. Slow growth in the rest of the world and the relative strength of the dollar also held down net exports. Largely as a result of these factors, the economy contracted at a 0.2 percent annual rate during the first quarter. (At the time the economic assumptions were finalized, the Bureau of Economic Analysis (BEA) estimated a larger 0.7 percent decline.)

Following the temporary disruption in growth caused by these idiosyncratic factors, and assuming adoption of the President's proposed fiscal plan, the Administration projects economic growth to rebound in the second quarter and remain above trend during the second half of 2015 and through 2018. With strong labor market performance since the Budget economic assumptions were finalized in November, the Administration now projects a more rapid decline in the unemployment rate in the near term and also projects lower unemployment rates during the 10-year budget window than projected in the 2016 Budget.

## Table 2. ECONOMIC ASSUMPTIONS[1]

(Calendar years; dollar amounts in billions)

| | Actual | | | Projections | | | | | | | | | |
|---|---|---|---|---|---|---|---|---|---|---|---|---|---|
| | 2013 | 2014 | 2015 | 2016 | 2017 | 2018 | 2019 | 2020 | 2021 | 2022 | 2023 | 2024 | 2025 |
| **Gross Domestic Product (GDP):** | | | | | | | | | | | | | |
| Levels, dollar amounts in billions: | | | | | | | | | | | | | |
| Current dollars | 16,768 | 17,419 | 17,941 | 18,762 | 19,626 | 20,527 | 21,416 | 22,350 | 23,322 | 24,335 | 25,392 | 26,494 | 27,645 |
| Real, chained (2009) dollars | 15,710 | 16,086 | 16,429 | 16,915 | 17,396 | 17,860 | 18,277 | 18,698 | 19,128 | 19,568 | 20,018 | 20,478 | 20,949 |
| Chained price index (2009 = 100), annual average | 106.7 | 108.3 | 109.2 | 110.9 | 112.9 | 115.0 | 117.2 | 119.6 | 122.0 | 124.4 | 126.9 | 129.4 | 132.0 |
| Percent change, fourth quarter over fourth quarter: | | | | | | | | | | | | | |
| Current dollars | 4.6 | 3.7 | 3.0 | 4.6 | 4.7 | 4.4 | 4.3 | 4.4 | 4.3 | 4.3 | 4.3 | 4.3 | 4.3 |
| Real, chained (2009) dollars | 3.1 | 2.4 | 2.0 | 2.9 | 2.8 | 2.5 | 2.3 | 2.3 | 2.3 | 2.3 | 2.3 | 2.3 | 2.3 |
| Chained price index (2009 = 100) | 1.4 | 1.2 | 1.1 | 1.6 | 1.8 | 1.9 | 2.0 | 2.0 | 2.0 | 2.0 | 2.0 | 2.0 | 2.0 |
| Percent change, year over year: | | | | | | | | | | | | | |
| Current dollars | 3.7 | 3.9 | 3.0 | 4.6 | 4.6 | 4.6 | 4.3 | 4.4 | 4.3 | 4.3 | 4.3 | 4.3 | 4.3 |
| Real, chained (2009) dollars | 2.2 | 2.4 | 2.1 | 3.0 | 2.8 | 2.7 | 2.3 | 2.3 | 2.3 | 2.3 | 2.3 | 2.3 | 2.3 |
| Chained price index (2009 = 100) | 1.5 | 1.5 | 0.8 | 1.6 | 1.7 | 1.9 | 2.0 | 2.0 | 2.0 | 2.0 | 2.0 | 2.0 | 2.0 |
| **Incomes, billions of current dollars:** | | | | | | | | | | | | | |
| Domestic corporate profits | 1,704 | 1,696 | 1,778 | 1,835 | 1,854 | 1,873 | 1,900 | 1,958 | 2,018 | 2,060 | 2,112 | 2,162 | 2,217 |
| Employee compensation | 8,845 | 9,228 | 9,625 | 10,011 | 10,455 | 10,938 | 11,443 | 11,966 | 12,518 | 13,100 | 13,710 | 14,363 | 15,003 |
| Wages and salaries | 7,125 | 7,452 | 7,764 | 8,080 | 8,447 | 8,851 | 9,258 | 9,678 | 10,116 | 10,581 | 11,072 | 11,600 | 12,121 |
| Other taxable income[2] | 4,012 | 4,146 | 4,278 | 4,501 | 4,734 | 5,019 | 5,295 | 5,574 | 5,880 | 6,180 | 6,476 | 6,763 | 7,055 |
| **Consumer Price Index (all urban):[3]** | | | | | | | | | | | | | |
| Level (1982–84 = 100), annual average | 233.0 | 236.7 | 237.3 | 241.8 | 246.5 | 251.8 | 257.4 | 263.2 | 269.2 | 275.3 | 281.5 | 287.9 | 294.4 |
| Percent change, fourth quarter over fourth quarter | 1.2 | 1.2 | 0.8 | 1.9 | 2.1 | 2.2 | 2.3 | 2.3 | 2.3 | 2.3 | 2.3 | 2.3 | 2.3 |
| Percent change, year over year | 1.5 | 1.6 | 0.2 | 1.9 | 2.0 | 2.1 | 2.2 | 2.3 | 2.3 | 2.3 | 2.3 | 2.3 | 2.3 |
| **Unemployment rate, civilian, percent:** | | | | | | | | | | | | | |
| Fourth quarter level | 7.0 | 5.7 | 5.1 | 4.7 | 4.6 | 4.6 | 4.8 | 4.9 | 4.9 | 4.9 | 4.9 | 4.9 | 4.9 |
| Annual average | 7.4 | 6.2 | 5.3 | 4.9 | 4.6 | 4.6 | 4.7 | 4.8 | 4.9 | 4.9 | 4.9 | 4.9 | 4.9 |
| **Federal pay raises, January, percent:** | | | | | | | | | | | | | |
| Military[4] | 1.7 | 1.0 | 1.0 | 1.3 | NA | NA | NA | NA | NA | NA | NA | NA | NA |
| Civilian[5] | 0.0 | 1.0 | 1.0 | 1.3 | NA | NA | NA | NA | NA | NA | NA | NA | NA |
| **Interest rates, percent:** | | | | | | | | | | | | | |
| 91-day Treasury bills[6] | 0.1 | * | 0.1 | 0.5 | 1.2 | 1.9 | 2.6 | 3.1 | 3.2 | 3.2 | 3.2 | 3.2 | 3.2 |
| 10-year Treasury notes | 2.4 | 2.5 | 2.2 | 2.9 | 3.5 | 3.9 | 4.1 | 4.3 | 4.3 | 4.4 | 4.4 | 4.4 | 4.4 |

\* 0.05 percent or less.

NA = Not Available

[1] Based on information available as of late May 2015.

[2] Rent, interest, dividend, and proprietors' income components of personal income.

[3] Seasonally adjusted CPI for all urban consumers.

[4] Percentages apply to basic pay only; percentages to be proposed for years after 2016 have not yet been determined.

[5] Overall average increase, including locality pay adjustments. Percentages to be proposed for years after 2016 have not yet been determined.

[6] Average rate, secondary market (bank discount basis).

Beyond the medium term (four to six years), the Administration's forecast is based on the long-run trends expected for real GDP growth, the unemployment rate, price inflation, and interest rates. Projected real GDP growth in the long run is below the historical average for the United States because of an expected decline in the growth of the labor force as the baby-boom generation retires.

## ECONOMIC PROJECTIONS

The MSR economic projections are based on information available on June 2, and assume adoption of the policies in the President's Budget. The projections are summarized in Table 2.

*Real Gross Domestic Product (GDP):* Real GDP is expected to rise by 2.0 percent during the four quarters of 2015, and then to rebound to 2.9 percent for 2016, followed by deceleration to 2.8 percent during 2017 and 2.5 percent during 2018 as the economy reaches full employment. The average growth rate from 2014-2019 is somewhat below what was published in the Budget, because of the downward revision for 2015 GDP. Beyond 2018, real GDP growth is projected to moderate. The growth rate is steady at 2.3 percent per year in 2020-2025, the same as in the Budget.

*Unemployment:* The unemployment rate is projected to reach 5.1 percent by the fourth quarter of 2015, two-tenths of a percentage point below its level in June. With continued economic growth and accommodative monetary policy, the unemployment rate is projected to dip to 4.6 percent in 2017-18 before settling at 4.9 percent, the rate consistent with stable inflation in the long run. During the period when the unemployment rate is below 4.9 percent, the rate of inflation is expected to converge to the Federal Reserve target. Inflation was 1.2 percent as measured by the core PCE price index during the 12 months through May, and it is expected to gradually increase to the Federal Reserve target of 2.0 percent, and then to stabilize there. The unemployment rate is projected to stabilize at a slightly lower level than that projected in the 2016 Budget forecast. The downward revision reflects a reassessment of the determinants of the rate of unemployment consistent with stable inflation in the long run, taking into account demographic changes, for example.

*Inflation:* Recently, overall inflation, as measured by the consumer price index (CPI), has been well below the Federal Open Market Committee's (FOMC) 2 percent target partly due to the rapid drop in oil prices. (The difference is even larger, considering that the Federal Reserve has framed its inflation expectation in terms of the price index for personal consumption expenditures, a price index that tends to run 0.25 percentage point less than the CPI.) However, core CPI inflation (that is, excluding food and energy prices) has been fairly stable around a level modestly below 2 percent. In the long run, the overall CPI inflation rate is projected to be 2.25 percent per year (2.3 percent with rounding), unchanged from the Budget projection. (As discussed above, the forecast of 2.3 percent for CPI inflation is consistent with 2.0 percent inflation for the price index for personal consumption expenditures.) The chained price index for gross domestic product, another key measure of inflation, is projected to increase by 1.1 percent during the four quarters of 2015, with the rate of change rising steadily to 2.0 percent by 2019 and then staying at that rate through the forecast horizon.

*Interest Rates:* The projections for interest rates are based on financial market data, market expectations, and surveys of economic forecasters at the time the forecast was completed. The three-month Treasury bill rate is expected to average only 0.1 percent in 2015. It is expected to begin to rise in 2015 and to reach 3.2 percent in 2021. The yield on the 10-year Treasury note is expected to average 2.2 percent in 2015 and to rise to 4.4 percent in 2022. The ultimate level of the three-month Treasury rate is 24 basis points less than projected in the Budget, while the 10-year rate is 10 basis points less than previously projected. This change is informed by further analysis of market data and historical trends and is consistent with a downward revision to the consensus forecast of private economists.

*Incomes and Income Shares:* During the economic recovery, corporate profits rebounded more quickly than labor compensation (which consists of wages and salaries and employee fringe benefits) while interest rates remained low. As a result, corporate profits have risen as a share of total income, while the labor compensation share is below its long-run average. As the economy recovers fully, some of this shift in shares is expected to reverse. Labor compensation and interest payments are projected to rise somewhat relative to total income, while the corporate profits share is projected to fall. The wage share (which excludes fringe benefits) also is expected to recover from its recent low level in step with the increase in total compensation. The wage share of GDP is slightly higher in this forecast than in the Budget forecast reflecting a higher jump-off level of wage and salary income and gross domestic income relative to GDP in the first quarter of 2015.

## FORECAST COMPARISONS

Comparisons of the MSR forecast with the Budget, and with the June Blue Chip consensus (an average of about 50 private-sector forecasts), the Congressional Budget Office (CBO), and the FOMC forecasts from June are shown below in Table 3. The Administration's GDP forecast is very close to the Blue Chip consensus. The Administration and Blue Chip both forecast 2.0 percent for real GDP growth during the four quarters of 2015 and 2.3 percent for the growth rate of real GDP in the final five years of the Budget window, and the 10-year average is 2.4 percent in both forecasts. The Administration's GDP forecast is higher than those of CBO and FOMC, in part because of the assumption that the Congress will enact the policies proposed in the President's 2016 Budget.

The Administration projects that unemployment will decline to 5.1 percent in the fourth quarter of 2015, and to 4.7 percent at the end of 2016. In comparison to the Administration forecast, the June Blue Chip consensus is the same for the fourth quarter of 2015 and slightly higher for the fourth quarter of 2016. The FOMC also projects that unemployment will fall. By the fourth quarter of 2016, the central tendency of the FOMC forecast is the range between 4.9 percent and 5.1 percent. (The CBO projections – last updated in January – assumed a higher trajectory for the unemployment rate, but do not reflect favorable labor market developments over the past several months, during which Blue Chip and FOMC revised their 2015 unemployment forecasts downward.)

The Administration projects inflation and interest rates that are similar to the Blue Chip consensus in the long run. These Administration forecasts are slightly below those forecasts by the CBO. Since the last CBO forecast was finalized in December and published in January, lower-than-expected inflation has led many forecasters to lower inflation and interest rate forecasts.

### Table 3. COMPARISON OF ECONOMIC ASSUMPTIONS
(Calendar years; dollar amounts in billions)

| | 2014 | 2015 | 2016 | 2017 | 2018 | 2019 | 2020 | 2021 | 2022 | 2023 | 2024 | 2025 |
|---|---|---|---|---|---|---|---|---|---|---|---|---|
| **Nominal GDP:** | | | | | | | | | | | | |
| MSR | 17,419 | 17,941 | 18,762 | 19,626 | 20,527 | 21,416 | 22,350 | 23,322 | 24,335 | 25,392 | 26,494 | 27,645 |
| Budget | 17,394 | 18,188 | 19,039 | 19,933 | 20,847 | 21,770 | 22,717 | 23,705 | 24,736 | 25,812 | 26,934 | 28,106 |
| CBO | 17,422 | 18,204 | 19,045 | 19,919 | 20,768 | 21,625 | 22,550 | 23,515 | 24,515 | 25,550 | 26,625 | 27,736 |
| Blue Chip[1] | 17,419 | 17,979 | 18,838 | 19,747 | 20,686 | 21,648 | 22,633 | 23,636 | 24,688 | 25,786 | 26,933 | 28,131 |
| | | | | *percent change, fourth quarter over fourth quarter* | | | | | | | | |
| **Real GDP:** | | | | | | | | | | | | |
| MSR | 2.4 | 2.0 | 2.9 | 2.8 | 2.5 | 2.3 | 2.3 | 2.3 | 2.3 | 2.3 | 2.3 | 2.3 |
| Budget | 2.1 | 3.0 | 3.0 | 2.7 | 2.5 | 2.3 | 2.3 | 2.3 | 2.3 | 2.3 | 2.3 | 2.3 |
| CBO | 2.1 | 2.9 | 2.9 | 2.5 | 2.1 | 2.1 | 2.2 | 2.2 | 2.2 | 2.1 | 2.1 | 2.1 |
| Blue Chip[1] | 2.4 | 2.0 | 2.7 | 2.7 | 2.5 | 2.3 | 2.4 | 2.3 | 2.3 | 2.3 | 2.3 | 2.3 |
| FOMC[2] | | 1.8-2.0 | 2.4-2.7 | 2.1-2.5 | | | 2.0 to 2.3 'longer run' | | | | | |

## Table 3. COMPARISON OF ECONOMIC ASSUMPTIONS—Continued

(Calendar years; dollar amounts in billions)

|  | 2014 | 2015 | 2016 | 2017 | 2018 | 2019 | 2020 | 2021 | 2022 | 2023 | 2024 | 2025 |
|---|---|---|---|---|---|---|---|---|---|---|---|---|
| | | | | | *percent change, year over year* | | | | | | | |
| **Real GDP:** | | | | | | | | | | | | |
| MSR | 2.4 | 2.1 | 3.0 | 2.8 | 2.7 | 2.3 | 2.3 | 2.3 | 2.3 | 2.3 | 2.3 | 2.3 |
| Budget | 2.2 | 3.1 | 3.0 | 2.8 | 2.6 | 2.4 | 2.3 | 2.3 | 2.3 | 2.3 | 2.3 | 2.3 |
| CBO | 2.3 | 2.8 | 3.0 | 2.7 | 2.2 | 2.1 | 2.2 | 2.2 | 2.2 | 2.1 | 2.1 | 2.1 |
| Blue Chip | 2.4 | 2.2 | 2.8 | 2.7 | 2.6 | 2.4 | 2.4 | 2.3 | 2.3 | 2.3 | 2.3 | 2.3 |
| **GDP Price Index:** | | | | | | | | | | | | |
| MSR | 1.5 | 0.8 | 1.6 | 1.7 | 1.9 | 2.0 | 2.0 | 2.0 | 2.0 | 2.0 | 2.0 | 2.0 |
| Budget | 1.5 | 1.4 | 1.6 | 1.8 | 2.0 | 2.0 | 2.0 | 2.0 | 2.0 | 2.0 | 2.0 | 2.0 |
| CBO | 1.6 | 1.6 | 1.6 | 1.9 | 2.0 | 2.0 | 2.0 | 2.0 | 2.0 | 2.0 | 2.1 | 2.0 |
| Blue Chip | 1.5 | 1.0 | 1.9 | 2.1 | 2.1 | 2.2 | 2.1 | 2.1 | 2.1 | 2.1 | 2.1 | 2.1 |
| **Consumer Price Index (CPI-U):** | | | | | | | | | | | | |
| MSR | 1.6 | 0.2 | 1.9 | 2.0 | 2.1 | 2.2 | 2.3 | 2.3 | 2.3 | 2.3 | 2.3 | 2.3 |
| Budget | 1.7 | 1.4 | 1.9 | 2.1 | 2.2 | 2.3 | 2.3 | 2.3 | 2.3 | 2.3 | 2.3 | 2.3 |
| CBO | 1.7 | 1.1 | 2.2 | 2.3 | 2.4 | 2.4 | 2.4 | 2.4 | 2.4 | 2.4 | 2.4 | 2.4 |
| Blue Chip | 1.6 | 0.2 | 2.2 | 2.3 | 2.4 | 2.4 | 2.4 | 2.3 | 2.2 | 2.2 | 2.2 | 2.2 |
| | | | | | *annual average in percent* | | | | | | | |
| **Unemployment Rate:** | | | | | | | | | | | | |
| MSR | 6.2 | 5.3 | 4.9 | 4.6 | 4.6 | 4.7 | 4.8 | 4.9 | 4.9 | 4.9 | 4.9 | 4.9 |
| Budget | 6.2 | 5.4 | 5.1 | 4.9 | 4.9 | 5.0 | 5.1 | 5.2 | 5.2 | 5.2 | 5.2 | 5.2 |
| CBO | 6.2 | 5.6 | 5.4 | 5.3 | 5.4 | 5.5 | 5.5 | 5.5 | 5.4 | 5.4 | 5.4 | 5.4 |
| Blue Chip | 6.2 | 5.3 | 4.9 | 4.9 | 5.0 | 5.0 | 5.0 | 5.1 | 5.1 | 5.1 | 5.1 | 5.1 |
| FOMC[3] | | 5.2-5.3 | 4.9-5.1 | 4.9-5.1 | | | 5.0 to 5.2 'longer run' | | | | | |
| **Interest Rates:** | | | | | | | | | | | | |
| *91-Day Treasury Bills (discount basis):* | | | | | | | | | | | | |
| MSR | * | 0.1 | 0.5 | 1.2 | 1.9 | 2.6 | 3.1 | 3.2 | 3.2 | 3.2 | 3.2 | 3.2 |
| Budget | * | 0.4 | 1.6 | 2.4 | 2.9 | 3.2 | 3.3 | 3.4 | 3.4 | 3.5 | 3.5 | 3.5 |
| CBO | * | 0.2 | 1.2 | 2.6 | 3.5 | 3.4 | 3.4 | 3.4 | 3.4 | 3.4 | 3.4 | 3.4 |
| Blue Chip | * | 0.2 | 1.2 | 2.7 | 3.2 | 3.3 | 3.4 | 3.4 | 3.4 | 3.4 | 3.4 | 3.4 |
| *10-Year Treasury Notes:* | | | | | | | | | | | | |
| MSR | 2.5 | 2.2 | 2.9 | 3.5 | 3.9 | 4.1 | 4.3 | 4.3 | 4.4 | 4.4 | 4.4 | 4.4 |
| Budget | 2.6 | 2.8 | 3.3 | 3.7 | 4.0 | 4.3 | 4.5 | 4.5 | 4.5 | 4.5 | 4.5 | 4.5 |
| CBO | 2.6 | 2.8 | 3.4 | 3.9 | 4.2 | 4.5 | 4.6 | 4.6 | 4.6 | 4.6 | 4.6 | 4.6 |
| Blue Chip | 2.5 | 2.2 | 3.0 | 3.9 | 4.2 | 4.3 | 4.3 | 4.3 | 4.4 | 4.4 | 4.4 | 4.4 |

* 0.05 percent or less.

MSR = 2016 Mid-Session Review (forecast date: June 2015)

Budget = 2016 Budget (forecast date: November 2014)

CBO = Congressional Budget Office January 2015 baseline economic forecast

FOMC = Federal Reserve Open Market Committee (forecast central tendency date: June 17, 2015)

Blue Chip = June 2015 Blue Chip Consensus Forecast extended with March 2015 Blue Chip long-run survey (publication date: June 10, 2015)

Sources: Administration; Federal Open Market Committee *Projections Materials*, June 17, 2015; *Blue Chip Economic Indicators*, March and June 2015, Aspen Publishers; CBO, The Budget and Economic Outlook: January 2015

[1] Values for 2017–2025 interpolated by OMB from annual growth rates.

[2] The FOMC's central tendency for longer term growth is 2.0% to 2.3%. Longer-run represents each participant's assessment of the rate to which GDP growth would be expected to converge under appropriate monetary policy and in the absence of further shocks to the economy.

[3] Fourth quarter levels of unemployment.

# RECEIPTS

The Mid-Session Review (MSR) estimates of receipts are above the 2016 Budget estimates by $72 billion in 2015 and by $32 billion in 2016. In each subsequent year, the MSR estimates of receipts are below the Budget estimates by $15 billion to $86 billion, for a decrease in receipts of $539 billion over the 10-year budget horizon (2016 through 2025).

The net increase in 2015 receipts is in large part attributable to technical revisions based on new tax reporting data, collections to date, and other information, which increase receipts by $95 billion. Revised economic assumptions partially offset this increase, reducing 2015 receipts by $22 billion.

The estimate of 2016 receipts is also above the Budget estimate because a $60 billion increase in receipts attributable to technical factors is only partially offset by a $27 billion reduction in receipts attributable to revised economic assumptions.

The $539 billion reduction in receipts over the 10-year budget horizon is largely the result of a $590 billion loss in receipts attributable to revisions in the economic forecast. A reduction in the net gain in receipts from the Administration's proposals reduces receipts by an additional $40 billion. These reductions are partially offset by technical revisions and enacted legislation, which increase receipts by $90 billion and $2 billion, respectively.

## ECONOMIC CHANGES

Revisions in the economic forecast reduce receipts by $22 billion in 2015, $27 billion in 2016, and $43 billion to $74 billion in each subsequent year, for a total reduction of $590 billion over the 10 years from 2016 through 2025. In 2015, revisions to the economic forecast have the greatest effect on individual and corporation income taxes, reducing those sources of receipts by $6 billion and $15 billion, respectively. The reduction in individual income taxes is primarily attributable to reductions in the forecast of proprietors' income. Changes in the forecasts of GDP and other economic measures that affect the profitability of corporations are primarily responsible for the reduction in 2015 corporation income taxes.

Over the 10-year budget horizon, revisions in the economic forecast have the greatest effect on corporation income taxes, reducing collections by $234 billion. The reduction is driven by net reductions in estimates of taxable corporate income relative to the Budget forecast due to downward revisions in the forecast of GDP, which are only partially offset by reductions in the forecast of wages and salaries (which are treated as deductions to corporate income). Revisions in the economic forecast also reduce collections of individual income taxes and social insurance and retirement receipts, reducing 10-year collections by $231 billion and $163 billion, respectively. Reductions in the economic forecasts of wages and salaries and nonwage sources of personal income are primarily responsible for the reduction in individual income taxes. Reductions in the forecasts of wages and salaries and proprietors' income, which are the tax base for Social Security and Medicare payroll taxes, the largest components of social insurance and retirement receipts, account for most of the reduction in this source of receipts. Revisions in the forecasts of GDP, interest rates, imports, and other sources of income increase all remaining sources of receipts by a net $38 billion.

## TECHNICAL CHANGES

Technical revisions in the estimates of receipts increase receipts by $95 billion in 2015, $60 billion in 2016, $32 billion in 2017, and smaller amounts in each year, 2018 through 2021. Technical revisions reduce receipts by $2 billion to $10 billion in each subsequent year, for a net increase of $90 billion over the 10 years, 2016 through 2025. Technical revisions increase collections of individual income taxes and social insurance and retirement receipts by $120 billion and $67 billion, respectively, over the 10-year budget horizon. These net increases reflect more recent collections data, revisions in estimating models based on updated tax and other data, and the gains in receipts due to the November 2014 immigration executive actions. In contrast, more recent collections data and revisions in the corporation income tax model reduce collections of corporation income taxes by a net $85 billion. Technical revisions in all other sources of receipts (excise taxes, customs duties, estate and gift taxes, deposits of earnings of the Federal Reserve System, and penalties and fees) result in a net 10-year reduction in receipts of $12 billion.

## ENACTED LEGISLATION AND REVISIONS IN PROVISIONS EXTENDED IN THE ADJUSTED BASELINE AND PROPOSALS

Relative to the estimates in the Budget, legislation enacted since the Budget was completed has had only a modest impact on receipts, increasing 10-year collections by $2 billion.[1]

The adjusted baseline permanently continues the American Opportunity Tax Credit and improvements to the Child Tax Credit and Earned Income Tax Credit that were initially enacted in the American Recovery and Reinvestment Act of 2009 and extended through tax year 2017 under the American Taxpayer Relief Act of 2012. There is little change in the 10-year cost of extending these provisions.

Revisions in the estimates of the net savings from the Administration's proposals reduce receipts by $40 billion over the 10 years, 2016 through 2025. Revisions in the placeholder for the effect on receipts of the Administration's immigration reform proposal, which has been revised to reflect the Congressional Budget Office's March 2015 reestimate of immigration reform, account for $36 billion of this reduction in receipts. (Additional information on the placeholder is contained in the "Expenditures" section of this MSR.) The remaining $4 billion reduction in receipts reflects small revisions in the estimates of a number of provisions and the receipt impact of the Administration's recently-transmitted proposal to establish a blended military retirement system, as discussed in the next section.

---

[1] The Trade Preference Extension Act of 2015 (P.L. 114-27), which enacted a number of Administration proposals, including extensions of the African Growth and Opportunity Act, the Generalized System of Preferences, and Trade Adjustment Assistance, was enacted too late to be included in the MSR estimates.

RECEIPTS

## Table 4. CHANGE IN RECEIPTS
(In billions of dollars)

| | 2015 | 2016 | 2017 | 2018 | 2019 | 2020 | 2021 | 2022 | 2023 | 2024 | 2025 | 2016-2020 | 2016-2025 |
|---|---|---|---|---|---|---|---|---|---|---|---|---|---|
| **2016 Budget estimate** | 3,176 | 3,525 | 3,755 | 3,944 | 4,135 | 4,332 | 4,525 | 4,746 | 4,986 | 5,236 | 5,478 | | |
| Changes in current law receipts due to revised economic assumptions: | | | | | | | | | | | | | |
| Individual income taxes | –6 | –6 | –15 | –20 | –21 | –24 | –25 | –28 | –31 | –29 | –32 | –86 | –231 |
| Corporation income taxes | –15 | –31 | –34 | –32 | –26 | –20 | –16 | –17 | –18 | –20 | –21 | –143 | –234 |
| Social insurance and retirement | * | –4 | –12 | –13 | –15 | –17 | –19 | –20 | –22 | –21 | –21 | –60 | –163 |
| Other | –1 | 14 | 18 | 12 | 1 | –1 | –1 | –1 | –1 | –1 | –* | 44 | 38 |
| Total, changes due to revised economic assumptions | –22 | –27 | –43 | –53 | –62 | –61 | –62 | –65 | –73 | –71 | –74 | –246 | –590 |
| Changes in current law receipts due to technical reestimates: | | | | | | | | | | | | | |
| Individual income taxes | 69 | 59 | 34 | 18 | 9 | 9 | 4 | 1 | –2 | –6 | –6 | 128 | 120 |
| Corporation income taxes | 20 | –14 | –10 | –12 | –12 | –10 | –9 | –7 | –6 | –4 | –* | –58 | –85 |
| Social insurance and retirement | 5 | 13 | 7 | 8 | 8 | 8 | 7 | 6 | 4 | 3 | 3 | 44 | 67 |
| Other | * | 1 | 1 | 1 | –* | –1 | –2 | –2 | –3 | –3 | –5 | 2 | –12 |
| Total, changes due to technical reestimates | 95 | 60 | 32 | 14 | 5 | 5 | 1 | –2 | –6 | –10 | –9 | 116 | 90 |
| Changes in current law receipts due to enacted legislation | * | * | * | 1 | * | * | * | * | * | * | * | 2 | 2 |
| Changes in provisions extended in the adjusted baseline due to economic and technical revisions | | | | * | * | –* | * | –* | –* | –* | –* | * | –* |
| Changes in proposals due to enacted legislation and economic and technical revisions: | | | | | | | | | | | | | |
| Enact comprehensive immigration reform | | –1 | –5 | –8 | –9 | –5 | –2 | | | –3 | –3 | –28 | –36 |
| Proposed blended military retirement system | | | | –* | –* | –* | –* | –* | –* | –* | –* | –* | –2 |
| Other proposals | –1 | * | 1 | –* | –2 | –* | 1 | –1 | –1 | –1 | –* | –1 | –3 |
| Total, changes in proposals | –1 | –1 | –4 | –8 | –11 | –5 | –1 | –1 | –1 | –4 | –3 | –30 | –40 |
| Total change in receipts | 72 | 32 | –15 | –46 | –67 | –62 | –62 | –69 | –79 | –84 | –86 | –158 | –539 |
| **2016 Mid-Session estimate** | 3,248 | 3,557 | 3,740 | 3,898 | 4,068 | 4,270 | 4,463 | 4,677 | 4,906 | 5,152 | 5,392 | | |

\* $500 million or less.

# EXPENDITURES

Outlays for 2015 in the Mid-Session Review (MSR) are estimated to be $3,703 billion, $56 billion lower than the 2016 Budget estimate, reflecting slower-than-expected spending across a range of discretionary and mandatory programs. Projected outlays have fallen by $13 billion in 2016 relative to the Budget, and by $401 billion over the 10-year budget horizon, 2016 to 2025. These decreases in spending are primarily the cumulative effect of economic and technical reestimates in a number of mandatory programs and net interest, as well as lower debt service associated with the changes in outlays and receipts.

## ENACTED LEGISLATION AND REVISIONS IN PROPOSALS

Relative to the estimates in the Budget, legislation enacted since the Budget was completed has had a modest impact on outlays. In 2015, enacted legislation decreases spending by $0.1 billion relative to the 2016 Budget policy levels. Enacted legislation continues to have a minimal effect on spending over the next 10 years, 2016 through 2025, increasing outlays by $9 billion over that time period.[1]

The Medicare Access and CHIP Reauthorization Act of 2015 (P.L. 114-10), enacted in April, accounts for nearly all of the changes due to enacted legislation. This bill replaced the sustainable growth rate formula with specified annual updates to fee-for-service payment rates for physicians' services in Medicare, established incentives to encourage Medicare providers to participate in alternate payment models, extended funding for the Children's Health Insurance Program (CHIP) through 2017, and made permanent a subsidy of Part B premiums for certain low-income Medicare beneficiaries. It temporarily extended other expiring provisions related to Medicare and Medicaid, along with certain other programs. To partially offset the budgetary cost of these provisions, the bill reduced updates to Medicare's payment rates for services furnished by providers of post-acute care, increased premiums paid by higher-income Medicare enrollees, prohibited Medicare Supplemental Insurance policies from covering the Part B deductible for new beneficiaries beginning in 2020, and temporarily modified hospital payments.

In addition, three proposals submitted to the Congress by the Administration since publication of the Budget have modest impacts on estimated outlays. The Administration reviewed recommendations by the Military Compensation and Retirement Modernization Commission and submitted legislative proposals to offer a blended military retirement system and provide appropriate retirement benefits to survivors, and to sunset the Chapter 30 Montgomery GI Bill for Active Duty and the Chapter 1607 Reserve Educational Assistance Program to reduce redundancy with Post-9/11 GI Bill benefits. These three proposals will decrease discretionary outlays for military personnel benefits by $7 billion over 10 years, and they will increase scoreable mandatory outlays by $1 billion while reducing non-scoreable mandatory accrual receipts by $17 billion over the same period.

## ESTIMATING CHANGES

Estimating changes are due to factors other than enacted legislation or changes in proposals. These result from changes in economic assumptions, discussed earlier in this MSR, and changes in technical factors. Relative to the Budget estimates, economic and technical changes decrease estimated outlays for 2015 by $56 billion, and decrease outlays by $430 billion from 2016 through 2025.

**Discretionary programs.** Outlays for discretionary programs decrease by $23 billion in 2015 but rise by $23 billion over the next 10 years relative to the Budget as a result of technical revisions. These changes reflect lower outlays in 2015 compared to the Budget for both defense and non-defense discretionary programs, due to slower-than-expected spending patterns. Of the $23 bil-

---

[1] The Trade Preference Extension Act of 2015 (P.L. 114-27), which enacted a number of Administration proposals, including extensions of the African Growth and Opportunity Act, the Generalized System of Preferences, and Trade Adjustment Assistance, was enacted too late to be included in the MSR estimates.

lion reduction in 2015, $5 billion is the net reduction in outlays for defense programs and overseas contingency operations, primarily reflecting slower-than-expected outlays for military personnel and in a variety of investment accounts, partially offset by faster-than-expected outlays in operation and maintenance accounts. The remaining $19 billion reduction is in non-defense programs, most notably in the Department of Housing and Urban Development, due to slower-than-anticipated outlays and higher-than-expected Federal Housing Administration forward mortgage loan volume, and the Department of Homeland Security, due to lower-than-anticipated disaster events.

**Social Security.** Estimating changes reduce outlays for Social Security by $7 billion in 2015 and by an additional $229 billion over the next 10 years. The reduction for 2016 through 2025 is almost entirely due to the MSR's lower forecast for the Consumer Price Index, which results in lower cost-of-living adjustments for 2016 through 2020. The reduction in 2015 is due primarily to incorporating recent data showing lower-than-expected numbers of beneficiaries starting benefits at younger ages. These reductions continue through the early years of the budget window, adding to the outlay reductions due to lower COLAs. In later years, the decreases in awards at younger ages lead to increases in awards at higher ages, an effect which partially offsets the decreases due to economic assumptions.

**Medicare.** Economic and technical changes increase outlays for Medicare by $7 billion in 2015, and by $97 billion over the next 10 years. Technical changes include increases in Parts A and B spending due to an increased rate of beneficiary enrollment in Medicare Advantage and higher actual expenditure data in certain service lines compared to previous estimates. In addition, projected slower growth of market basket and price indices result in decreased outlays relative to the Budget. Increases in Part D are due to the net effect of lower-than-estimated enrollment, an increase in expected drug spending, particularly on specialty drugs such as Hepatitis C treatments and new cholesterol drugs, and higher-than-estimated average drug rebates.

**Premium tax credit and cost-sharing reductions.** Changes in technical assumptions and the incorporation of recent data from the marketplaces for the refundable portion of the premium tax credit and related payments for cost sharing reductions reduce net outlays by $3 billion in 2015, and increase net outlays by $59 billion (or 6.3 percent) from 2016 through 2025. This increase in outlays is partially offset by $5 billion in increased receipts attributable to the premium tax credit, for a net increase of $54 billion when outlay and revenue effects are taken into account.

**Immigration reform.** Outlays from the Budget's placeholder for comprehensive immigration reform are reduced by $48 billion from 2016 to 2025, based on the Congressional Budget Office's March 2015 reestimate of immigration reform. (Additional information on the placeholder is contained in the "Revenues" section of this MSR.)

**Unemployment compensation.** Changes in economic and technical assumptions decrease outlays for unemployment benefits by $4 billion in 2015. From 2016 through 2025, estimated outlays are reduced by an additional $41 billion relative to the Budget estimate. The reduction is driven in large part by continued decline in insured unemployment rates relative to the overall unemployment rate as well as lower near-term civilian unemployment rates and a smaller labor force than was assumed in the President's Budget. In addition, lower actual spending in recent months than had been assumed in the Budget contributes to the downward revision in spending during the budget window.

**Medicaid.** Technical and economic revisions increase projected Federal outlays for Medicaid by $14 billion in 2015 relative to the Budget estimates, and further increase outlays by $39 billion over 2016 to 2025. The increase stems primarily from an increase in projected Medicaid per enrollee spending and enrollment. Economic factors partially offset this increase as a reduction in wage growth, the Consumer Price Index, and other medical economic indicators decrease costs.

**Veterans programs.** Outlays for mandatory veterans programs decrease by $3 billion in 2015, and by $22 billion from 2016 to 2025. In part, this decrease results from lower cost-of-living adjustments. In addition, participation in the new Veterans Choice Program has been lower than anticipated in 2015.

**Civilian and military retirement.** Projected outlays for civilian and military retirement have increased by $1 billion in 2015, and by $18 billion from 2016 to 2025, due primarily to higher average annuity projections for civilian retirement, partially offset by lower projected cost-of-living adjustments for both programs.

**Child Tax Credit (CTC).** Estimating changes decrease outlays for the CTC by $1 billion in 2015 and increase outlays by $17 billion from 2016 through 2025. The increase results from improved modeling of the income distribution for taxpayers eligible for the credit.

**Supplemental Security Income (SSI).** Outlays for SSI decrease by $1 billion in 2015, and further decrease by $16 billion from 2016 to 2025, largely due to lower cost-of-living projections which result in lower benefit payments, along with fewer projected recipients.

**Federal Employee Health Benefits Program (FEHB).** Net outlays for the FEHB revolving fund increase by $11 billion over the next 10 years from 2016 to 2025. Premium receipts have been lower following the last open season. In addition, year-to-date activity has demonstrated higher-than-anticipated payments to experience-rated carriers, particularly the expenses of the Service Benefit Plan. Finally, the revised MSR economic forecast projects lower interest rates on the purchase of new securities, resulting in lower projected interest earnings over that period.

**Earned Income Tax Credit (EITC).** Estimating changes increase outlays for the EITC by $11 billion from 2016 through 2025. This is the net effect of decreased outlays relative to the Budget due to a lower projected unemployment rate that causes fewer beneficiaries to be projected to stay within the income eligibility requirements for shorter periods of time, and increased outlays from various technical changes.

**Supplemental Nutrition Assistance Program (SNAP).** Outlays for SNAP decrease by $10 billion over the next 10 years relative to the Budget due to economic and technical factors, including lower projections of participation based on actual participation in recent months.

**Crop insurance.** Outlays for crop insurance decrease by $2 billion in 2015, due to a lower actual loss-ratio through May 2015 than was assumed in the Budget. An increase of $8 billion from 2016 to 2025 is due to an increase in commodity price projections provided by the U.S. Department of Agriculture's World Agriculture Outlook Board in May 2015.

**Child Nutrition.** Child Nutrition outlays increase by $7 billion over the next 10 years. Faster-than-anticipated increases in participation, likely due to expansion of the Community Eligibility Provision that streamlines certification, counting, and claiming procedures in low-income school districts, explains over two-thirds of the increase. The price index assumption for food away from home has increased compared to the Budget, further increasing outlays.

**Pension Benefit Guaranty Corporation (PBGC).** Net outlays for PBGC decrease by $1 billion in 2015, and increase by $6 billion between 2016 and 2025. These changes primarily result from a lower assumed interest rate, as well as updates and refinements to the models PBGC uses to project single-employer and multiemployer program outlays.

**Higher education.** Mandatory higher education outlays decrease by $8 billion in 2015, and decrease by an additional $5 billion for 2016 through 2025. The majority of the decrease in 2015 results from a revision to the reestimate of the cost of direct student loan originations in past years, partially offset by the effect of changes in estimates of volume for loan originations in the current year. Lower-than-expected 2014-2015 Pell grant award levels contribute to the decrease in 2015 and the forecast for 2016 and beyond. Lower cost-of-living adjustments lead to additional decreases in program costs in the outyears.

**Foreign Military Sales (FMS) Trust Fund.** Outlays for the FMS Trust Fund decrease by $4 billion in 2015, due to reduced sales estimates and slower-than-expected expenditures for existing large sales.

**Proceeds from Government Sponsored Enterprises (GSEs).** The current-year forecast for GSE proceeds has been updated to reflect actual dividends received for the most recent two quarters, through the third quarter of 2015, leading to a $6 billion decrease in receipts in 2015 relative to the Budget. This change is the result of lower valuations for financial derivatives that the companies hold to hedge against interest rate risk and does not represent a deterioration in housing market conditions. The estimated fair value of the GSEs' derivatives may fluctuate substantially from quarter to quarter because of changes in interest rates and other factors. The value of these investments in turn affects the GSEs' net worth, which forms the basis for the GSEs' quarterly dividend payments to Treasury.

**Net interest.** Excluding the debt service associated with enacted legislation and policy changes, outlays for net interest are projected to decrease by $19 billion in 2015 and by $393 billion over the next 10 years. The majority of the reduction, $340 billion, is the result of revised economic assumptions, including lower interest rate and Consumer Price Index assumptions. Technical revisions of $17 billion reflect actual data through May for marketable and nonmarketable securities and through March for other actuals, revised estimates of interest transactions with credit financing accounts, and updated projections of other transactions affecting borrowing from the public. Debt service on all changes in receipts and outlays compared to the Budget reduces interest outlays by $34 billion.

# Table 5. CHANGE IN OUTLAYS

(In billions of dollars)

| | 2015 | 2016 | 2017 | 2018 | 2019 | 2020 | 2021 | 2022 | 2023 | 2024 | 2025 | 2016-2020 | 2016-2025 |
|---|---|---|---|---|---|---|---|---|---|---|---|---|---|
| **2016 Budget estimate** | 3,759 | 3,999 | 4,218 | 4,423 | 4,653 | 4,886 | 5,126 | 5,372 | 5,621 | 5,875 | 6,165 | | |
| Changes due to enacted legislation and policy changes: | | | | | | | | | | | | | |
| Medicare Access and CHIP Reauthorization Act of 2015 | * | –1 | 4 | 2 | –2 | –1 | –* | * | 2 | 2 | 4 | 1 | 8 |
| Other enacted legislation | –* | * | * | * | * | * | * | * | * | * | * | * | 1 |
| Proposals to reflect Military Compensation and Retirement Modernization Commission recommendations: | | | | | | | | | | | | | |
| Scoreable effect | | * | * | * | * | * | * | * | * | * | * | 1 | 1 |
| Non-scoreable and discretionary effects | | * | * | 1 | 1 | 2 | 2 | 2 | 2 | 3 | 3 | 4 | 16 |
| Debt service | –* | –* | * | * | * | * | * | * | * | 1 | 1 | * | 3 |
| Subtotal, enacted legislation and policy changes | –* | –1 | 4 | 3 | –1 | 1 | 2 | 3 | 5 | 5 | 8 | 6 | 29 |
| Changes due to reestimates: | | | | | | | | | | | | | |
| Discretionary appropriations: | | | | | | | | | | | | | |
| Defense base programs | –5 | –* | 4 | 5 | 4 | 2 | 1 | 1 | 1 | 1 | 1 | 14 | 19 |
| Non-defense base programs | –19 | 2 | 1 | 1 | * | –* | * | –* | * | –* | * | 4 | 5 |
| Overseas contingency operations | 1 | –* | –* | * | * | | | | | | | –* | –* |
| Subtotal, discretionary appropriations | –23 | 1 | 5 | 6 | 4 | 2 | 2 | 1 | 1 | 1 | 1 | 18 | 23 |
| Social Security | –7 | –14 | –19 | –21 | –22 | –24 | –24 | –25 | –25 | –26 | –27 | –100 | –229 |
| Medicare | 7 | 1 | 9 | 12 | 9 | 10 | 10 | 11 | 13 | 11 | 12 | 41 | 97 |
| Premium tax credits and cost-sharing reductions | –3 | –* | 6 | 7 | 5 | 6 | 7 | 7 | 7 | 7 | 8 | 24 | 59 |
| Immigration reform | | –3 | –1 | –3 | –4 | –8 | –4 | –5 | –6 | –8 | –6 | –19 | –48 |
| Unemployment compensation | –4 | –3 | –3 | –4 | –4 | –4 | –4 | –4 | –5 | –5 | –5 | –18 | –41 |
| Medicaid | 14 | 30 | 5 | 2 | 3 | 2 | 1 | * | –1 | –1 | –1 | 41 | 39 |
| Veterans programs | –3 | –1 | –1 | –2 | –2 | –2 | –3 | –3 | –3 | –3 | –3 | –8 | –22 |
| Civilian and military retirement | 1 | 1 | 1 | 1 | 1 | 2 | 2 | 2 | 2 | 2 | 3 | 7 | 18 |
| Child Tax Credit | –1 | 1 | 1 | 1 | 2 | 2 | 2 | 2 | 2 | 2 | 2 | 7 | 17 |
| Supplemental Security Income | –1 | –1 | –1 | –1 | –2 | –2 | –2 | –2 | –2 | –2 | –2 | –7 | –16 |
| Federal Employee Health Benefits Program | * | 1 | 1 | 1 | 1 | 1 | 1 | 1 | 1 | 2 | 1 | 5 | 11 |
| Earned Income Tax Credit | * | 2 | 3 | 2 | 3 | 2 | –* | * | 1 | –* | –1 | 12 | 11 |
| Supplemental Nutritional Assistance Program | | –1 | –1 | –1 | –1 | –1 | –1 | –1 | –1 | –* | –1 | –5 | –10 |
| Crop insurance | –2 | –* | –* | 1 | 1 | 1 | 1 | 1 | 1 | 1 | 1 | 2 | 8 |
| Child Nutrition | –* | 1 | 1 | 1 | 1 | 1 | 1 | 1 | 1 | 1 | 1 | 3 | 7 |
| Pension Benefit Guaranty Corporation | –1 | * | * | 1 | 1 | 1 | 1 | 1 | 1 | 1 | 1 | 3 | 6 |
| Higher education | –8 | 1 | –* | –* | –1 | –1 | –1 | –1 | –1 | –1 | –1 | –1 | –5 |
| Foreign Military Sales Trust Fund | –4 | | | | | | | | | | | | |
| Proceeds from Government-Sponsored Enterprises | 6 | | | | | | | | | | | | |
| Other programs [1] | –10 | 5 | 6 | 11 | 4 | * | 1 | –7 | –3 | 15 | 4 | 26 | 35 |
| Net interest [2] | –19 | –33 | –56 | –59 | –50 | –41 | –36 | –33 | –31 | –28 | –25 | –239 | –393 |
| Subtotal, reestimates | –56 | –12 | –45 | –47 | –51 | –54 | –48 | –54 | –48 | –33 | –39 | –208 | –430 |
| Total change in outlays | –56 | –13 | –41 | –44 | –51 | –53 | –46 | –51 | –43 | –28 | –31 | –202 | –401 |
| **Mid-Session estimate** | 3,703 | 3,987 | 4,177 | 4,379 | 4,601 | 4,833 | 5,080 | 5,320 | 5,578 | 5,847 | 6,134 | | |

*$500 million or less.

[1] Includes change in allowance for future disaster costs.

[2] Includes debt service on all reestimates.

# SUMMARY TABLES

## Table S–1. BUDGET TOTALS
(In billions of dollars and as a percent of GDP)

| | 2014 | 2015 | 2016 | 2017 | 2018 | 2019 | 2020 | 2021 | 2022 | 2023 | 2024 | 2025 | Totals 2016-2020 | Totals 2016-2025 |
|---|---|---|---|---|---|---|---|---|---|---|---|---|---|---|
| **Budget Totals in Billions of Dollars:** | | | | | | | | | | | | | | |
| Receipts | 3,021 | 3,248 | 3,557 | 3,740 | 3,898 | 4,068 | 4,270 | 4,463 | 4,677 | 4,906 | 5,152 | 5,392 | 19,534 | 44,125 |
| Outlays | 3,506 | 3,703 | 3,987 | 4,177 | 4,379 | 4,601 | 4,833 | 5,080 | 5,320 | 5,578 | 5,847 | 6,134 | 21,978 | 49,937 |
| Deficit | 485 | 455 | 429 | 436 | 481 | 533 | 563 | 617 | 643 | 672 | 695 | 742 | 2,443 | 5,812 |
| Debt held by the public | 12,780 | 13,411 | 13,974 | 14,541 | 15,152 | 15,810 | 16,493 | 17,221 | 17,973 | 18,754 | 19,556 | 20,404 | | |
| Debt net of financial assets | 11,455 | 11,910 | 12,339 | 12,775 | 13,256 | 13,789 | 14,351 | 14,967 | 15,610 | 16,281 | 16,976 | 17,717 | | |
| Gross domestic product (GDP) | 17,263 | 17,806 | 18,554 | 19,404 | 20,305 | 21,190 | 22,113 | 23,075 | 24,078 | 25,124 | 26,214 | 27,353 | | |
| **Budget Totals as a Percent of GDP:** | | | | | | | | | | | | | | |
| Receipts | 17.5% | 18.2% | 19.2% | 19.3% | 19.2% | 19.2% | 19.3% | 19.3% | 19.4% | 19.5% | 19.7% | 19.7% | 19.2% | 19.4% |
| Outlays | 20.3% | 20.8% | 21.5% | 21.5% | 21.6% | 21.7% | 21.9% | 22.0% | 22.1% | 22.2% | 22.3% | 22.4% | 21.6% | 21.9% |
| Deficit | 2.8% | 2.6% | 2.3% | 2.2% | 2.4% | 2.5% | 2.5% | 2.7% | 2.7% | 2.7% | 2.7% | 2.7% | 2.4% | 2.5% |
| Debt held by the public | 74.0% | 75.3% | 75.3% | 74.9% | 74.6% | 74.6% | 74.6% | 74.6% | 74.6% | 74.6% | 74.6% | 74.6% | | |
| Debt net of financial assets | 66.4% | 66.9% | 66.5% | 65.8% | 65.3% | 65.1% | 64.9% | 64.9% | 64.8% | 64.8% | 64.8% | 64.8% | | |

## Table S-2. EFFECT OF BUDGET PROPOSALS ON PROJECTED DEFICITS

(Deficit increases (+) or decreases (−) in billions of dollars)

| | 2015 | 2016 | 2017 | 2018 | 2019 | 2020 | 2021 | 2022 | 2023 | 2024 | 2025 | Totals 2016-2020 | Totals 2016-2025 |
|---|---|---|---|---|---|---|---|---|---|---|---|---|---|
| **Projected deficits in the adjusted baseline**[1] | 448 | 495 | 528 | 547 | 668 | 743 | 795 | 966 | 1,006 | 1,014 | 1,189 | 2,982 | 7,952 |
| Percent of GDP | 2.5% | 2.7% | 2.7% | 2.7% | 3.2% | 3.4% | 3.4% | 4.0% | 4.0% | 3.9% | 4.3% | 2.9% | 3.4% |
| **Proposals in the 2016 MSR:**[2] | | | | | | | | | | | | | |
| **Tax reforms and investments to support working families:** | | | | | | | | | | | | | |
| Middle-class and pro-work tax reforms | ...... | 11 | 27 | 28 | 28 | 28 | 29 | 30 | 31 | 32 | 33 | 121 | 277 |
| Child care for all low- and moderate-income families with young children | ...... | 3 | 4 | 5 | 6 | 7 | 8 | 9 | 11 | 12 | 14 | 24 | 78 |
| Partner with States to provide tuition-free quality community college | ...... | * | 1 | 2 | 3 | 5 | 6 | 8 | 9 | 12 | 13 | 12 | 60 |
| Capital gains tax reform | ...... | −12 | −24 | −20 | −21 | −22 | −22 | −24 | −25 | −26 | −28 | −99 | −225 |
| Financial fee | ...... | −6 | −11 | −11 | −11 | −11 | −12 | −12 | −12 | −12 | −13 | −50 | −111 |
| Proposals to address high-income tax avoidance[3] | ...... | −5 | −8 | −8 | −8 | −9 | −9 | −10 | −11 | −11 | −11 | −38 | −90 |
| Debt service | ...... | −* | −* | −* | −1 | −1 | −1 | −1 | −1 | −1 | −1 | −2 | −8 |
| Total, tax reforms and investments to support working families | ...... | −9 | −11 | −4 | −5 | −4 | −1 | * | 2 | 5 | 9 | −33 | −18 |
| **Additional investments in growing the economy and creating opportunity:** | | | | | | | | | | | | | |
| Surface transportation reauthorization | ...... | 5 | 12 | 15 | 17 | 18 | 19 | 16 | 10 | 6 | 4 | 67 | 121 |
| Transition revenue from business tax reform[4] | ...... | −34 | −56 | −54 | −52 | −50 | −20 | ...... | ...... | ...... | ...... | −247 | −266 |
| Investments in early education and children's health[5] | ...... | * | 1 | 5 | 9 | 7 | 10 | 11 | 12 | 12 | 11 | 23 | 80 |
| Tobacco tax financing | ...... | −8 | −10 | −10 | −10 | −10 | −9 | −9 | −8 | −8 | −7 | −49 | −91 |
| Additional investments in education, innovation, infrastructure, and security | ...... | 37 | 51 | 57 | 56 | 49 | 40 | −20 | −46 | −60 | −69 | 250 | 95 |
| Additional mandatory and tax proposals | 1 | −32 | −15 | 22 | −27 | −32 | −36 | −98 | −47 | 15 | −48 | −84 | −298 |
| Debt service | * | −* | −* | −1 | −1 | −1 | −1 | −3 | −6 | −9 | −11 | −2 | −34 |
| Total, additional investments | 1 | −32 | −18 | 34 | −8 | −19 | 2 | −102 | −86 | −43 | −121 | −42 | −393 |
| **Additional deficit reduction from health, tax, and immigration reform:** | | | | | | | | | | | | | |
| Health savings[6] | 6 | 4 | −10 | −17 | −22 | −31 | −40 | −49 | −57 | −69 | −75 | −77 | −367 |
| Reforms to high-income tax expenditures[7] | ...... | −35 | −46 | −52 | −58 | −64 | −68 | −73 | −78 | −83 | −88 | −254 | −644 |
| Immigration reform | ...... | 4 | 3 | −5 | −10 | −20 | −20 | −25 | −29 | −34 | −34 | −28 | −170 |
| Debt service | * | −* | −1 | −2 | −5 | −10 | −15 | −21 | −27 | −34 | −42 | −17 | −156 |
| Total, additional deficit reduction | 6 | −27 | −54 | −76 | −95 | −125 | −143 | −168 | −191 | −220 | −239 | −377 | −1,337 |
| **Subtotal, tax reforms, investments, and additional deficit reduction** | 6 | −68 | −83 | −46 | −108 | −148 | −143 | −270 | −275 | −258 | −351 | −452 | −1,748 |
| **Other changes to deficits:** | | | | | | | | | | | | | |
| Reductions in Overseas Contingency Operations | ...... | −11 | −30 | −41 | −48 | −51 | −54 | −71 | −81 | −85 | −87 | −181 | −559 |
| Replacement of mandatory sequestration | ...... | 11 | 18 | 19 | 19 | 20 | 21 | 22 | 28 | 31 | 1 | 87 | 190 |

## Table S–2. EFFECT OF BUDGET PROPOSALS ON PROJECTED DEFICITS—Continued

(Deficit increases (+) or decreases (−) in billions of dollars)

|  | 2015 | 2016 | 2017 | 2018 | 2019 | 2020 | 2021 | 2022 | 2023 | 2024 | 2025 | Totals 2016-2020 | Totals 2016-2025 |
|---|---|---|---|---|---|---|---|---|---|---|---|---|---|
| Proposed Budget Control Act cap adjustment for disaster relief and wildfires | ……… | 2 | 2 | 3 | 3 | 1 | 1 | 1 | 1 | 1 | 1 | 12 | 18 |
| Debt service and indirect interest effects | * | –* | –* | –1 | –1 | –2 | –4 | –5 | –7 | –9 | –12 | –5 | –41 |
| Total, other changes to deficit | * | 2 | –9 | –20 | –27 | –32 | –35 | –53 | –59 | –62 | –97 | –87 | –392 |
| **Total proposals in the 2016 MSR** | **6** | **–66** | **–92** | **–66** | **–135** | **–180** | **–178** | **–323** | **–334** | **–320** | **–447** | **–539** | **–2,141** |
| **Resulting deficits in the 2016 MSR** | **455** | **429** | **436** | **481** | **533** | **563** | **617** | **643** | **672** | **695** | **742** | **2,443** | **5,812** |
| Percent of GDP | 2.6% | 2.3% | 2.2% | 2.4% | 2.5% | 2.5% | 2.7% | 2.7% | 2.7% | 2.7% | 2.7% | 2.4% | 2.5% |
| **Memorandum:** | | | | | | | | | | | | | |
| **Debt held by the public in the adjusted baseline** | 13,405 | 14,028 | 14,676 | 15,342 | 16,123 | 16,972 | 17,864 | 18,930 | 20,035 | 21,143 | 22,423 | | |
| Percent of GDP | 75.3% | 75.6% | 75.6% | 75.6% | 76.1% | 76.8% | 77.4% | 78.6% | 79.7% | 80.7% | 82.0% | | |
| **Debt held by the public in the 2016 MSR** | 13,411 | 13,974 | 14,541 | 15,152 | 15,810 | 16,493 | 17,221 | 17,973 | 18,754 | 19,556 | 20,404 | | |
| Percent of GDP | 75.3% | 75.3% | 74.9% | 74.6% | 74.6% | 74.6% | 74.6% | 74.6% | 74.6% | 74.6% | 74.6% | | |

\* $500 million or less.

[1] See Tables S-4 and S-7 for information on the adjusted baseline.
[2] For total deficit reduction since January 2011, see Table S-3.
[3] Includes proposals to limit the total accrual of tax-favored retirement benefits and conform SECA taxes for professional service businesses.
[4] Business tax reform transition revenue of $266.3 billion finances the $126.5 billion in budget authority for new surface transportation investments (the PAYGO portion of the reauthorization proposal) plus $111.9 billion of cash transfers necessary to ensure Transportation Trust Fund solvency for all programs proposed to be funded via the Transportation Trust Fund over the six-year reauthorization period, leaving an additional $27.9 billion for deficit reduction.
[5] Includes proposals to support preschool for all, extend the Maternal, Infant, and Early Childhood Home Visiting program, and extend CHIP funding through 2019.
[6] Includes all HHS health savings and OPM FEHBP savings.
[7] Includes proposals to reduce the value of certain tax expenditures and implement the Buffett Rule by imposing a new "Fair Share Tax."

## Table S-3. CUMULATIVE DEFICIT REDUCTION
(Deficit reduction (–) or increase (+) in billions of dollars)

| | 2016–2025 |
|---|---:|
| **Deficit reduction achieved through July 2015, excluding Overseas Contingency Operations (OCO):** | |
| Enacted deficit reduction excluding pending Joint Committee enforcement: | |
|   Discretionary savings [1] | –1,634 |
|   Mandatory savings | –97 |
|   Revenues | –776 |
|   Debt service | –848 |
|   Subtotal, enacted deficit reduction excluding pending Joint Committee enforcement | –3,355 |
| Pending Joint Committee enforcement: [2] | |
|   Discretionary cap reductions | –533 |
|   Mandatory sequestration | –190 |
|   Debt service | –154 |
|   Subtotal, pending Joint Committee enforcement | –877 |
| Total, deficit reduction achieved, excluding OCO | –4,232 |
| **Tax reforms and investments to support working families:** | |
| Tax reform and investment proposals [3] | –11 |
| Debt service | –8 |
| Total, tax reforms and investments to support working families | –18 |
| **Additional investments in growing the economy and creating opportunity:** | |
| Investment proposals and offsets [4] | –360 |
| Debt service | –34 |
| Total, additional investments | –393 |
| **Additional deficit reduction from health, tax, and immigration reform:** | |
| Health savings | –367 |
| Reforms to high-income tax expenditures | –644 |
| Immigration reform | –170 |
| Debt service | –156 |
| Total, additional deficit reduction | –1,337 |
| **Subtotal, tax reforms, investments, and additional deficit reduction** | **–1,748** |
| **Other changes to deficits:** [1] | |
| Replacement of mandatory sequestration | 190 |
| Proposed Budget Control Act cap adjustment for disaster relief and wildfires | 18 |
| Debt service and indirect interest effects | 35 |
| Total, other changes to deficits | 243 |
| **Grand total, achieved and proposed deficit reduction excluding OCO** | **–5,738** |

## Table S–3. CUMULATIVE DEFICIT REDUCTION—Continued
(Deficit reduction (–) or increase (+) in billions of dollars)

| | 2016–2025 |
|---|---|
| **Memorandum: revenue and outlay effects of achieved and proposed deficit reduction:** | |
| Enacted outlay reductions and 2016 Budget spending proposals | –3,354 |
| Enacted receipt increases and 2016 Budget tax proposals | –2,213 |
| Immigration reform | –170 |
| **Memorandum, savings in Overseas Contingency Operations (OCO):** | |
| Enacted reduction in OCO funding | –1,016 |
| Proposed reductions in OCO | –559 |
| Debt service | –347 |
| Total, savings in overseas contingency operations (OCO) | **–1,921** |

[1] Excludes savings from reductions in OCO.
[2] Consists of mandatory sequestration for 2016–2024 and discretionary cap reductions for 2016–2021.
[3] See Table S–2 for details on tax reform and investment proposals.
[4] See Table S–2 for details on additional investment proposals.

## Table S-4. ADJUSTED BASELINE BY CATEGORY[1]
(In billions of dollars)

| | 2014 | 2015 | 2016 | 2017 | 2018 | 2019 | 2020 | 2021 | 2022 | 2023 | 2024 | 2025 | Totals 2016–2020 | Totals 2016–2025 |
|---|---|---|---|---|---|---|---|---|---|---|---|---|---|---|
| **Outlays:** | | | | | | | | | | | | | | |
| Appropriated ("discretionary") programs: | | | | | | | | | | | | | | |
| Defense | 596 | 584 | 631 | 663 | 670 | 677 | 688 | 700 | 718 | 735 | 753 | 771 | 3,328 | 7,006 |
| Non-defense | 525 | 539 | 565 | 570 | 571 | 576 | 584 | 595 | 607 | 621 | 635 | 650 | 2,866 | 5,975 |
| Subtotal, appropriated programs | 1,121 | 1,123 | 1,196 | 1,233 | 1,240 | 1,253 | 1,273 | 1,295 | 1,325 | 1,356 | 1,389 | 1,421 | 6,194 | 12,981 |
| Mandatory programs: | | | | | | | | | | | | | | |
| Social Security | 845 | 884 | 924 | 972 | 1,030 | 1,093 | 1,160 | 1,228 | 1,300 | 1,376 | 1,457 | 1,542 | 5,179 | 12,083 |
| Medicare | 505 | 537 | 589 | 607 | 614 | 676 | 730 | 785 | 882 | 915 | 942 | 1,048 | 3,215 | 7,786 |
| Medicaid | 301 | 341 | 370 | 369 | 387 | 408 | 427 | 449 | 473 | 500 | 529 | 561 | 1,960 | 4,471 |
| Other mandatory programs | 504 | 601 | 692 | 698 | 708 | 749 | 774 | 802 | 848 | 852 | 856 | 907 | 3,621 | 7,885 |
| Subtotal, mandatory programs | 2,156 | 2,363 | 2,575 | 2,646 | 2,738 | 2,927 | 3,090 | 3,264 | 3,504 | 3,642 | 3,783 | 4,057 | 13,975 | 32,226 |
| Net interest | 229 | 210 | 250 | 306 | 369 | 441 | 517 | 582 | 646 | 711 | 769 | 826 | 1,884 | 5,417 |
| Adjustments for disaster costs[2] | ......... | * | 3 | 7 | 8 | 9 | 9 | 10 | 10 | 10 | 10 | 10 | 36 | 86 |
| Joint Committee enforcement[3] | ......... | ......... | –66 | –96 | –104 | –107 | –108 | –108 | –56 | –40 | –35 | –3 | –480 | –723 |
| Total outlays | 3,506 | 3,697 | 3,958 | 4,095 | 4,252 | 4,523 | 4,781 | 5,042 | 5,428 | 5,679 | 5,915 | 6,312 | 21,609 | 49,985 |
| **Receipts:** | | | | | | | | | | | | | | |
| Individual income taxes | 1,395 | 1,540 | 1,663 | 1,725 | 1,813 | 1,903 | 2,011 | 2,125 | 2,245 | 2,367 | 2,494 | 2,623 | 9,115 | 20,968 |
| Corporation income taxes | 321 | 347 | 389 | 390 | 397 | 410 | 424 | 441 | 457 | 472 | 486 | 500 | 2,010 | 4,367 |
| Social insurance and retirement receipts: | | | | | | | | | | | | | | |
| Social Security payroll taxes | 736 | 771 | 805 | 837 | 877 | 916 | 953 | 1,003 | 1,052 | 1,097 | 1,150 | 1,199 | 4,388 | 9,889 |
| Medicare payroll taxes | 224 | 235 | 246 | 256 | 269 | 281 | 293 | 308 | 323 | 337 | 354 | 369 | 1,345 | 3,036 |
| Unemployment insurance | 55 | 55 | 54 | 52 | 52 | 49 | 50 | 50 | 50 | 51 | 52 | 52 | 257 | 512 |
| Other retirement | 9 | 10 | 10 | 10 | 11 | 11 | 12 | 12 | 13 | 14 | 14 | 15 | 54 | 122 |
| Excise taxes | 93 | 96 | 100 | 104 | 106 | 108 | 110 | 113 | 116 | 119 | 123 | 127 | 528 | 1,127 |
| Estate and gift taxes | 19 | 20 | 21 | 23 | 24 | 25 | 27 | 28 | 30 | 32 | 34 | 36 | 120 | 281 |
| Customs duties | 34 | 36 | 38 | 41 | 43 | 46 | 48 | 50 | 53 | 55 | 58 | 61 | 216 | 494 |
| Deposits of earnings, Federal Reserve System | 99 | 94 | 94 | 69 | 53 | 44 | 47 | 52 | 57 | 61 | 65 | 68 | 308 | 611 |
| Other miscellaneous receipts | 37 | 45 | 42 | 59 | 59 | 60 | 63 | 64 | 66 | 68 | 71 | 73 | 284 | 626 |
| Total receipts | 3,021 | 3,248 | 3,463 | 3,567 | 3,705 | 3,854 | 4,038 | 4,247 | 4,462 | 4,674 | 4,901 | 5,123 | 18,627 | 42,033 |
| **Deficit** | **485** | **448** | **495** | **528** | **547** | **668** | **743** | **795** | **966** | **1,006** | **1,014** | **1,189** | **2,982** | **7,952** |
| Net interest | 229 | 210 | 250 | 306 | 369 | 441 | 517 | 582 | 646 | 711 | 769 | 826 | 1,884 | 5,417 |
| **Primary deficit** | **256** | **238** | **246** | **222** | **178** | **227** | **226** | **213** | **320** | **295** | **246** | **363** | **1,099** | **2,535** |
| On-budget deficit | 514 | 475 | 512 | 531 | 535 | 637 | 683 | 720 | 871 | 879 | 862 | 1,003 | 2,898 | 7,234 |
| Off-budget deficit / surplus (–) | –30 | –27 | –17 | –3 | 12 | 31 | 60 | 75 | 95 | 126 | 152 | 186 | 84 | 719 |

## Table S–4. ADJUSTED BASELINE BY CATEGORY[1]—Continued
(In billions of dollars)

| | 2014 | 2015 | 2016 | 2017 | 2018 | 2019 | 2020 | 2021 | 2022 | 2023 | 2024 | 2025 | Totals 2016–2020 | Totals 2016–2025 |
|---|---|---|---|---|---|---|---|---|---|---|---|---|---|---|
| **Memorandum, budget authority for appropriated programs:[4]** | | | | | | | | | | | | | | |
| Defense | 606 | 586 | 642 | 657 | 671 | 685 | 701 | 716 | 734 | 752 | 770 | 789 | 3,357 | 7,117 |
| Non-defense | 523 | 526 | 537 | 547 | 559 | 572 | 584 | 596 | 611 | 626 | 641 | 657 | 2,798 | 5,930 |
| Total, appropriated funding | 1,129 | 1,112 | 1,179 | 1,203 | 1,230 | 1,257 | 1,285 | 1,313 | 1,345 | 1,377 | 1,411 | 1,446 | 6,155 | 13,046 |

\* $500 million or less.

[1] See Table S–7 for information on adjustments to the Balanced Budget and Emergency Deficit Control Act (BBEDCA) baseline.

[2] These amounts represent a placeholder for major disasters requiring Federal assistance for relief and reconstruction. Such assistance might be provided in the form of discretionary or mandatory outlays or tax relief. These amounts are included as outlays for convenience.

[3] Consists of mandatory sequestration for 2016–2024 and discretionary cap reductions for 2016–2021.

[4] Excludes discretionary cap reductions for Joint Committee enforcement.

## Table S-5. PROPOSED BUDGET BY CATEGORY
(In billions of dollars)

| | 2014 | 2015 | 2016 | 2017 | 2018 | 2019 | 2020 | 2021 | 2022 | 2023 | 2024 | 2025 | Totals 2016-2020 | Totals 2016-2025 |
|---|---|---|---|---|---|---|---|---|---|---|---|---|---|---|
| **Outlays:** | | | | | | | | | | | | | | |
| Appropriated ("discretionary") programs: | | | | | | | | | | | | | | |
| Defense | 596 | 584 | 604 | 598 | 587 | 585 | 590 | 596 | 608 | 621 | 634 | 647 | 2,964 | 6,071 |
| Non-defense | 525 | 539 | 565 | 582 | 587 | 592 | 594 | 599 | 594 | 597 | 608 | 619 | 2,921 | 5,938 |
| Subtotal, appropriated programs | 1,121 | 1,123 | 1,169 | 1,180 | 1,174 | 1,177 | 1,184 | 1,195 | 1,202 | 1,219 | 1,242 | 1,266 | 5,885 | 12,009 |
| Mandatory programs: | | | | | | | | | | | | | | |
| Social Security | 845 | 884 | 924 | 973 | 1,030 | 1,092 | 1,158 | 1,226 | 1,298 | 1,374 | 1,455 | 1,539 | 5,177 | 12,069 |
| Medicare | 505 | 537 | 586 | 594 | 593 | 650 | 696 | 743 | 831 | 857 | 871 | 971 | 3,118 | 7,392 |
| Medicaid | 301 | 346 | 378 | 371 | 388 | 407 | 430 | 452 | 477 | 502 | 531 | 564 | 1,974 | 4,501 |
| Other mandatory programs | 504 | 602 | 672 | 738 | 806 | 813 | 833 | 867 | 857 | 911 | 981 | 973 | 3,861 | 8,450 |
| Allowance for immigration reform | | | 5 | 10 | 15 | 20 | 20 | 25 | 30 | 35 | 40 | 50 | 70 | 250 |
| Subtotal, mandatory programs | 2,156 | 2,369 | 2,564 | 2,685 | 2,832 | 2,982 | 3,137 | 3,314 | 3,492 | 3,680 | 3,879 | 4,097 | 14,200 | 32,662 |
| Net interest | 229 | 210 | 250 | 305 | 365 | 434 | 503 | 561 | 616 | 670 | 716 | 761 | 1,857 | 5,180 |
| Adjustments for disaster costs [1] | | * | 3 | 7 | 8 | 9 | 9 | 10 | 10 | 10 | 10 | 10 | 36 | 86 |
| Total outlays | 3,506 | 3,703 | 3,987 | 4,177 | 4,379 | 4,601 | 4,833 | 5,080 | 5,320 | 5,578 | 5,847 | 6,134 | 21,978 | 49,937 |
| **Receipts:** | | | | | | | | | | | | | | |
| Individual income taxes | 1,395 | 1,540 | 1,701 | 1,792 | 1,888 | 1,988 | 2,105 | 2,225 | 2,351 | 2,480 | 2,613 | 2,748 | 9,474 | 21,891 |
| Corporation income taxes | 321 | 347 | 429 | 455 | 458 | 469 | 482 | 468 | 466 | 481 | 495 | 509 | 2,293 | 4,712 |
| Social insurance and retirement receipts: | | | | | | | | | | | | | | |
| Social Security payroll taxes | 736 | 771 | 808 | 841 | 882 | 921 | 958 | 1,008 | 1,058 | 1,103 | 1,157 | 1,205 | 4,409 | 9,940 |
| Medicare payroll taxes | 224 | 235 | 247 | 258 | 271 | 284 | 296 | 311 | 326 | 341 | 357 | 373 | 1,356 | 3,064 |
| Unemployment insurance | 55 | 55 | 56 | 59 | 59 | 57 | 58 | 58 | 59 | 60 | 61 | 62 | 290 | 590 |
| Other retirement | 9 | 10 | 10 | 10 | 11 | 11 | 12 | 12 | 13 | 14 | 14 | 15 | 54 | 122 |
| Excise taxes | 93 | 96 | 111 | 119 | 121 | 123 | 125 | 127 | 129 | 132 | 135 | 139 | 597 | 1,259 |
| Estate and gift taxes | 19 | 20 | 21 | 30 | 32 | 35 | 37 | 41 | 44 | 48 | 52 | 56 | 155 | 396 |
| Customs duties | 34 | 36 | 36 | 40 | 43 | 46 | 48 | 50 | 52 | 55 | 58 | 61 | 213 | 489 |
| Deposits of earnings, Federal Reserve System | 99 | 94 | 94 | 69 | 53 | 44 | 47 | 52 | 57 | 61 | 65 | 68 | 308 | 611 |
| Other miscellaneous receipts | 37 | 45 | 43 | 60 | 60 | 61 | 64 | 65 | 67 | 69 | 71 | 73 | 287 | 632 |
| Allowance for immigration reform | | | 1 | 7 | 20 | 30 | 40 | 45 | 55 | 64 | 74 | 84 | 98 | 420 |
| Total receipts | 3,021 | 3,248 | 3,557 | 3,740 | 3,898 | 4,068 | 4,270 | 4,463 | 4,677 | 4,906 | 5,152 | 5,392 | 19,534 | 44,125 |
| **Deficit** | **485** | **455** | **429** | **436** | **481** | **533** | **563** | **617** | **643** | **672** | **695** | **742** | **2,443** | **5,812** |
| Net interest | 229 | 210 | 250 | 305 | 365 | 434 | 503 | 561 | 616 | 670 | 716 | 761 | 1,857 | 5,180 |
| **Primary deficit / surplus (–)** | **256** | **244** | **180** | **132** | **116** | **100** | **60** | **56** | **27** | **2** | **–22** | **–19** | **586** | **631** |
| On-budget deficit | 514 | 482 | 452 | 442 | 470 | 508 | 509 | 549 | 556 | 554 | 552 | 565 | 2,380 | 5,156 |
| Off-budget deficit / surplus (–) | –30 | –28 | –23 | –5 | 11 | 26 | 54 | 67 | 87 | 118 | 143 | 177 | 63 | 655 |

## Table S–5. PROPOSED BUDGET BY CATEGORY—Continued
(In billions of dollars)

| | 2014 | 2015 | 2016 | 2017 | 2018 | 2019 | 2020 | 2021 | 2022 | 2023 | 2024 | 2025 | Totals 2016-2020 | Totals 2016-2025 |
|---|---|---|---|---|---|---|---|---|---|---|---|---|---|---|
| **Memorandum, budget authority for appropriated programs:** | | | | | | | | | | | | | | |
| Defense | 606 | 586 | 612 | 573 | 584 | 592 | 598 | 610 | 622 | 635 | 648 | 661 | 2,959 | 6,135 |
| Non-defense | 523 | 526 | 543 | 565 | 575 | 584 | 590 | 601 | 586 | 599 | 612 | 625 | 2,856 | 5,878 |
| Total, appropriated funding | 1,129 | 1,112 | 1,155 | 1,138 | 1,159 | 1,176 | 1,188 | 1,211 | 1,208 | 1,234 | 1,260 | 1,286 | 5,815 | 12,013 |

\* $500 million or less.

[1] These amounts represent a placeholder for major disasters requiring Federal assistance for relief and reconstruction. Such assistance might be provided in the form of discretionary or mandatory outlays or tax relief. These amounts are included as outlays for convenience.

## Table S–6. PROPOSED BUDGET BY CATEGORY AS A PERCENT OF GDP
(As a percent of GDP)

| | 2014 | 2015 | 2016 | 2017 | 2018 | 2019 | 2020 | 2021 | 2022 | 2023 | 2024 | 2025 | Averages 2016-2020 | Averages 2016-2025 |
|---|---|---|---|---|---|---|---|---|---|---|---|---|---|---|
| **Outlays:** | | | | | | | | | | | | | | |
| Appropriated ("discretionary") programs: | | | | | | | | | | | | | | |
| Defense | 3.5 | 3.3 | 3.3 | 3.1 | 2.9 | 2.8 | 2.7 | 2.6 | 2.5 | 2.5 | 2.4 | 2.4 | 2.9 | 2.7 |
| Non-defense | 3.0 | 3.0 | 3.0 | 3.0 | 2.9 | 2.8 | 2.7 | 2.6 | 2.5 | 2.4 | 2.3 | 2.3 | 2.9 | 2.6 |
| Subtotal, appropriated programs | 6.5 | 6.3 | 6.3 | 6.1 | 5.8 | 5.6 | 5.4 | 5.2 | 5.0 | 4.9 | 4.7 | 4.6 | 5.8 | 5.3 |
| Mandatory programs: | | | | | | | | | | | | | | |
| Social Security | 4.9 | 5.0 | 5.0 | 5.0 | 5.1 | 5.2 | 5.2 | 5.3 | 5.4 | 5.5 | 5.5 | 5.6 | 5.1 | 5.3 |
| Medicare | 2.9 | 3.0 | 3.2 | 3.1 | 2.9 | 3.1 | 3.1 | 3.2 | 3.5 | 3.4 | 3.3 | 3.6 | 3.1 | 3.2 |
| Medicaid | 1.7 | 1.9 | 2.0 | 1.9 | 1.9 | 1.9 | 1.9 | 2.0 | 2.0 | 2.0 | 2.0 | 2.1 | 1.9 | 2.0 |
| Other mandatory programs | 2.9 | 3.4 | 3.6 | 3.8 | 4.0 | 3.8 | 3.8 | 3.8 | 3.6 | 3.6 | 3.7 | 3.6 | 3.8 | 3.7 |
| Allowance for immigration reform | ........ | ........ | * | 0.1 | 0.1 | 0.1 | 0.1 | 0.1 | 0.1 | 0.1 | 0.2 | 0.2 | 0.1 | 0.1 |
| Subtotal, mandatory programs | 12.5 | 13.3 | 13.8 | 13.8 | 13.9 | 14.1 | 14.2 | 14.4 | 14.5 | 14.6 | 14.8 | 15.0 | 14.0 | 14.3 |
| Net interest | 1.3 | 1.2 | 1.3 | 1.6 | 1.8 | 2.0 | 2.3 | 2.4 | 2.6 | 2.7 | 2.7 | 2.8 | 1.8 | 2.2 |
| Adjustments for disaster costs[1] | ........ | * | * | * | * | * | * | * | * | * | * | * | * | * |
| Total outlays | 20.3 | 20.8 | 21.5 | 21.5 | 21.6 | 21.7 | 21.9 | 22.0 | 22.1 | 22.2 | 22.3 | 22.4 | 21.6 | 21.9 |
| **Receipts:** | | | | | | | | | | | | | | |
| Individual income taxes | 8.1 | 8.7 | 9.2 | 9.2 | 9.3 | 9.4 | 9.5 | 9.6 | 9.8 | 9.9 | 10.0 | 10.0 | 9.3 | 9.6 |
| Corporation income taxes | 1.9 | 1.9 | 2.3 | 2.3 | 2.3 | 2.2 | 2.2 | 2.0 | 1.9 | 1.9 | 1.9 | 1.9 | 2.3 | 2.1 |
| Social insurance and retirement receipts: | | | | | | | | | | | | | | |
| Social Security payroll taxes | 4.3 | 4.3 | 4.4 | 4.3 | 4.3 | 4.3 | 4.3 | 4.4 | 4.4 | 4.4 | 4.4 | 4.4 | 4.3 | 4.4 |
| Medicare payroll taxes | 1.3 | 1.3 | 1.3 | 1.3 | 1.3 | 1.3 | 1.3 | 1.3 | 1.4 | 1.4 | 1.4 | 1.4 | 1.3 | 1.3 |
| Unemployment insurance | 0.3 | 0.3 | 0.3 | 0.3 | 0.3 | 0.3 | 0.3 | 0.3 | 0.2 | 0.2 | 0.2 | 0.2 | 0.3 | 0.3 |
| Other retirement | 0.1 | 0.1 | 0.1 | 0.1 | 0.1 | 0.1 | 0.1 | 0.1 | 0.1 | 0.1 | 0.1 | 0.1 | 0.1 | 0.1 |
| Excise taxes | 0.5 | 0.5 | 0.6 | 0.6 | 0.6 | 0.6 | 0.6 | 0.6 | 0.5 | 0.5 | 0.5 | 0.5 | 0.6 | 0.6 |
| Estate and gift taxes | 0.1 | 0.1 | 0.1 | 0.2 | 0.2 | 0.2 | 0.2 | 0.2 | 0.2 | 0.2 | 0.2 | 0.2 | 0.2 | 0.2 |
| Customs duties | 0.2 | 0.2 | 0.2 | 0.2 | 0.2 | 0.2 | 0.2 | 0.2 | 0.2 | 0.2 | 0.2 | 0.2 | 0.2 | 0.2 |
| Deposits of earnings, Federal Reserve System | 0.6 | 0.5 | 0.5 | 0.4 | 0.3 | 0.3 | 0.2 | 0.2 | 0.3 | 0.3 | 0.3 | 0.3 | 0.3 | 0.3 |
| Other miscellaneous receipts | 0.2 | 0.3 | 0.2 | 0.3 | 0.3 | 0.3 | 0.3 | 0.3 | 0.3 | 0.3 | 0.3 | 0.3 | 0.3 | 0.3 |
| Allowance for immigration reform | ........ | ........ | * | * | 0.1 | 0.1 | 0.2 | 0.2 | 0.2 | 0.2 | 0.3 | 0.3 | 0.1 | 0.2 |
| Total receipts | 17.5 | 18.2 | 19.2 | 19.3 | 19.2 | 19.2 | 19.3 | 19.3 | 19.4 | 19.5 | 19.7 | 19.7 | 19.2 | 19.4 |
| **Deficit** | **2.8** | **2.6** | **2.3** | **2.2** | **2.4** | **2.5** | **2.5** | **2.7** | **2.7** | **2.7** | **2.7** | **2.7** | **2.4** | **2.5** |
| Net interest | 1.3 | 1.2 | 1.3 | 1.6 | 1.8 | 2.0 | 2.3 | 2.4 | 2.6 | 2.7 | 2.7 | 2.8 | 1.8 | 2.2 |
| **Primary deficit / surplus (–)** | **1.5** | **1.4** | **1.0** | **0.7** | **0.6** | **0.5** | **0.3** | **0.2** | **0.1** | ***** | **–0.1** | **–0.1** | **0.6** | **0.3** |
| On-budget deficit | 3.0 | 2.7 | 2.4 | 2.3 | 2.3 | 2.4 | 2.3 | 2.4 | 2.3 | 2.2 | 2.1 | 2.1 | 2.3 | 2.3 |
| Off-budget deficit / surplus (–) | –0.2 | –0.2 | –0.1 | –* | 0.1 | 0.1 | 0.2 | 0.3 | 0.4 | 0.5 | 0.5 | 0.6 | 0.1 | 0.3 |

## Table S–6. PROPOSED BUDGET BY CATEGORY AS A PERCENT OF GDP—Continued
(As a percent of GDP)

| | 2014 | 2015 | 2016 | 2017 | 2018 | 2019 | 2020 | 2021 | 2022 | 2023 | 2024 | 2025 | Averages 2016-2020 | Averages 2016-2025 |
|---|---|---|---|---|---|---|---|---|---|---|---|---|---|---|
| **Memorandum, budget authority for appropriated programs:** | | | | | | | | | | | | | | |
| Defense | 3.5 | 3.3 | 3.3 | 3.0 | 2.9 | 2.8 | 2.7 | 2.6 | 2.6 | 2.5 | 2.5 | 2.4 | 2.9 | 2.7 |
| Non-defense | 3.0 | 3.0 | 2.9 | 2.9 | 2.8 | 2.8 | 2.7 | 2.6 | 2.4 | 2.4 | 2.3 | 2.3 | 2.8 | 2.6 |
| Total, appropriated funding | 6.5 | 6.2 | 6.2 | 5.9 | 5.7 | 5.6 | 5.4 | 5.2 | 5.0 | 4.9 | 4.8 | 4.7 | 5.7 | 5.3 |

\*0.05 percent of GDP or less.

[1] These amounts represent a placeholder for major disasters requiring Federal assistance for relief and reconstruction. Such assistance might be provided in the form of discretionary or mandatory outlays or tax relief. These amounts are included as outlays for convenience.

## Table S–7. BRIDGE FROM BALANCED BUDGET AND EMERGENCY DEFICIT CONTROL ACT (BBEDCA) BASELINE TO ADJUSTED BASELINE

(Deficit increases (+) or decreases (–) in billions of dollars)

| | 2014 | 2015 | 2016 | 2017 | 2018 | 2019 | 2020 | 2021 | 2022 | 2023 | 2024 | 2025 | Totals 2016-2020 | Totals 2016-2025 |
|---|---|---|---|---|---|---|---|---|---|---|---|---|---|---|
| **BBEDCA baseline deficit** | 485 | 444 | 513 | 579 | 616 | 723 | 800 | 858 | 979 | 1,002 | 1,007 | 1,148 | 3,231 | 8,225 |
| **Adjustments for current policy:** | | | | | | | | | | | | | | |
| Continue tax benefits provided under the American Taxpayer Relief Act[1] | | | | | | 1 | 22 | 25 | 24 | 24 | 24 | 24 | 48 | 170 |
| Reflect incremental cost of funding existing Pell maximum grant award | | | 1 | 2 | 1 | 1 | 1 | * | * | –* | –* | –* | 5 | 5 |
| Reflect Postal Service default on retiree health benefit payments | | 3 | 7 | * | –* | –1 | –1 | –1 | –1 | –1 | –1 | –1 | 5 | 2 |
| Subtotal | | 3 | 7 | 2 | 2 | 2 | 22 | 24 | 24 | 24 | 23 | 23 | 58 | 177 |
| **Adjustments for provisions contained in the Budget Control Act:** | | | | | | | | | | | | | | |
| Set discretionary budget authority at cap levels[2] | | | 29 | 35 | 37 | 38 | 37 | 35 | 34 | 34 | 35 | 36 | 177 | 350 |
| Reflect Joint Committee enforcement[3] | | | –55 | –89 | –104 | –107 | –108 | –108 | –56 | –40 | –35 | –3 | –462 | –705 |
| Subtotal | | | –25 | –53 | –67 | –69 | –71 | –74 | –22 | –6 | –* | 33 | –285 | –355 |
| **Adjustments for emergency and disaster costs:** | | | | | | | | | | | | | | |
| Remove non-recurring emergency costs | | | –3 | –7 | –10 | –12 | –13 | –13 | –14 | –14 | –14 | –15 | –45 | –114 |
| Add placeholder for future emergency costs[4] | | * | 3 | 7 | 8 | 9 | 9 | 10 | 10 | 10 | 10 | 10 | 36 | 86 |
| **Reclassify surface transportation outlays:** | | | | | | | | | | | | | | |
| Remove outlays from appropriated category | –57 | –56 | –60 | –60 | –59 | –59 | –59 | –59 | –61 | –62 | –63 | –64 | –297 | –606 |
| Add outlays to mandatory category | 57 | 56 | 60 | 60 | 59 | 59 | 59 | 59 | 61 | 62 | 63 | 64 | 297 | 606 |
| Subtotal | | | | | | | | | | | | | | |
| Total program adjustments | | 4 | –17 | –51 | –67 | –51 | –51 | –54 | –2 | 14 | 19 | 51 | –236 | –207 |
| Debt service on adjustments | | –* | –* | –2 | –4 | –7 | –9 | –11 | –11 | –11 | –10 | –13 | –65 | |
| Total adjustments | | 4 | –17 | –51 | –68 | –55 | –57 | –63 | –13 | 3 | 8 | 41 | –249 | –273 |
| **Adjusted baseline deficit** | 485 | 448 | 495 | 528 | 547 | 668 | 743 | 795 | 966 | 1,006 | 1,014 | 1,189 | 2,982 | 7,952 |

\*$500 million or less.

[1] The baseline permanently continues the tax benefits provided to individuals and families that were extended only through taxable year 2017 under ATRA.

[2] Includes adjustments for discretionary and mandatory program integrity.

[3] Consists of mandatory sequestration for 2017-2024 and discretionary cap reductions for 2016-2021.

[4] These amounts represent a placeholder for major disasters requiring Federal assistance for relief and reconstruction.

SUMMARY TABLES 35

## Table S–8. MANDATORY AND RECEIPT PROPOSALS
(Deficit increases (+) or decreases (–) in millions of dollars)

| | 2015 | 2016 | 2017 | 2018 | 2019 | 2020 | 2021 | 2022 | 2023 | 2024 | 2025 | Totals 2016-2020 | Totals 2016-2025 |
|---|---|---|---|---|---|---|---|---|---|---|---|---|---|
| **Mandatory Initiatives and Savings:** | | | | | | | | | | | | | |
| Agriculture: | | | | | | | | | | | | | |
| Reduce premium subsidies for harvest price revenue protection and improve prevented planting coverage | ......... | –1,129 | –1,374 | –1,560 | –1,614 | –1,650 | –1,675 | –1,709 | –1,739 | –1,773 | –1,776 | –7,327 | –15,999 |
| Reauthorize Secure Rural Schools | ......... | ......... | 74 | 60 | 37 | 8 | ......... | ......... | ......... | ......... | ......... | 179 | 179 |
| Enact Food Safety and Inspection Service (FSIS) fee | ......... | –4 | –4 | –4 | –5 | –5 | –5 | –5 | –5 | –5 | –5 | –22 | –47 |
| Enact biobased labeling fee | ......... | ......... | ......... | ......... | ......... | ......... | ......... | ......... | ......... | ......... | ......... | ......... | ......... |
| Enact Grain Inspection, Packers, and Stockyards Administration (GIPSA) fee | ......... | –30 | –30 | –30 | –30 | –30 | –30 | –30 | –30 | –30 | –30 | –150 | –300 |
| Enact Animal Plant and Health Inspection Service (APHIS) fee | ......... | –20 | –27 | –27 | –28 | –29 | –30 | –31 | –32 | –33 | –34 | –131 | –291 |
| Enact Natural Resource and Conservation Service (NRCS) Conservation user fee | ......... | ......... | ......... | ......... | ......... | ......... | ......... | ......... | ......... | ......... | ......... | ......... | ......... |
| Establish Rural Housing Service (RHS) Guaranteed Underwriting System fee | ......... | ......... | 13 | 25 | 25 | 25 | 25 | 25 | 25 | 25 | 25 | 88 | 213 |
| Increase funding for Supplemental Nutrition Assistance Program (SNAP) Employment & Training [1] | ......... | ......... | ......... | ......... | ......... | ......... | ......... | ......... | ......... | ......... | ......... | ......... | ......... |
| Create State option to improve SNAP access for elderly | ......... | 9 | 21 | 34 | 41 | 48 | 54 | 60 | 67 | 74 | 80 | 153 | 488 |
| Out-year mandatory effects of discretionary changes to the Conservation Stewardship Program | ......... | ......... | ......... | –54 | –54 | –54 | –54 | –54 | –54 | –54 | –54 | –162 | –432 |
| Total, Agriculture | ......... | –1,174 | –1,327 | –1,556 | –1,628 | –1,687 | –1,715 | –1,744 | –1,768 | –1,796 | –1,794 | –7,372 | –16,189 |
| Commerce: | | | | | | | | | | | | | |
| Enact Scale Up Manufacturing Initiative | ......... | ......... | 163 | 365 | 365 | 365 | ......... | ......... | ......... | ......... | ......... | 1,258 | 1,258 |
| Expand National Network of Manufacturing Innovation | ......... | ......... | 90 | 190 | 280 | 390 | 390 | 290 | 200 | 100 | ......... | 950 | 1,930 |
| Total, Commerce | ......... | ......... | 253 | 555 | 645 | 755 | 390 | 290 | 200 | 100 | ......... | 2,208 | 3,188 |
| Education: | | | | | | | | | | | | | |
| Support Preschool for All | ......... | 130 | 1,235 | 3,110 | 5,456 | 7,360 | 8,773 | 9,787 | 10,560 | 10,275 | 9,356 | 17,291 | 66,042 |
| Enact Teaching for Tomorrow | ......... | 50 | 250 | 550 | 850 | 1,000 | 950 | 750 | 450 | 150 | ......... | 2,700 | 5,000 |
| Partner with States to provide tuition-free quality community college | ......... | 41 | 951 | 2,401 | 3,477 | 4,822 | 6,408 | 7,653 | 9,443 | 11,914 | 13,175 | 11,692 | 60,285 |
| Extend Pell CPI Increase | ......... | ......... | ......... | 226 | 1,104 | 2,055 | 3,044 | 4,095 | 5,208 | 6,389 | 7,624 | 3,385 | 29,745 |
| Reform student loan Income-Based Repayment plans [2] | ......... | –1,177 | –666 | –923 | –1,317 | –1,589 | –1,660 | –1,685 | –1,713 | –1,843 | –1,910 | –5,672 | –14,483 |
| Reform and expand Perkins loan program | ......... | –418 | –1,138 | –944 | –830 | –736 | –652 | –623 | –602 | –584 | –560 | –4,066 | –7,087 |
| Enact student aid reforms | ......... | –16 | –57 | –58 | –83 | –73 | –50 | –21 | 14 | 37 | 61 | –287 | –246 |
| Implement College Opportunity and Graduation Bonus Program | ......... | 123 | 360 | 481 | 671 | 684 | 692 | 702 | 709 | 719 | 727 | 2,319 | 5,868 |
| Total, Education | ......... | –1,267 | 935 | 4,843 | 9,328 | 13,523 | 17,505 | 20,658 | 24,069 | 27,057 | 28,473 | 27,362 | 145,124 |

## Table S-8. MANDATORY AND RECEIPT PROPOSALS—Continued

(Deficit increases (+) or decreases (−) in millions of dollars)

| | 2015 | 2016 | 2017 | 2018 | 2019 | 2020 | 2021 | 2022 | 2023 | 2024 | 2025 | Totals 2016-2020 | Totals 2016-2025 |
|---|---|---|---|---|---|---|---|---|---|---|---|---|---|
| **Energy:** | | | | | | | | | | | | | |
| Enact nuclear waste management program | ……… | ……… | ……… | ……… | 90 | 170 | 400 | 520 | 760 | −1,394 | 764 | 260 | 1,310 |
| Reauthorize special assessment from domestic nuclear utilities[3] | ……… | −204 | −208 | −213 | −218 | −223 | −228 | −233 | −238 | −244 | −249 | −1,066 | −2,258 |
| Establish Southwestern Power Administration Purchase Power Drought Fund | ……… | −15 | −15 | 5 | −15 | −2 | ……… | ……… | ……… | 24 | −15 | −42 | −33 |
| Total, Energy | ……… | −219 | −223 | −208 | −143 | −55 | 172 | 287 | 522 | −1,614 | 500 | −848 | −981 |
| **Health and Human Services:** | | | | | | | | | | | | | |
| **HHS health savings:** | | | | | | | | | | | | | |
| *Medicare providers:* | | | | | | | | | | | | | |
| Encourage delivery system reform: | | | | | | | | | | | | | |
| Make permanent the Medicare primary care incentive payment in a budget neutral manner | ……… | ……… | ……… | ……… | ……… | ……… | ……… | ……… | ……… | ……… | ……… | ……… | ……… |
| Encourage efficient care by improving incentives to provide care in the most appropriate ambulatory setting | ……… | ……… | −440 | −1,220 | −2,150 | −3,300 | −4,010 | −4,490 | −4,990 | −5,530 | −6,140 | −7,110 | −32,270 |
| Allow ACOs to pay beneficiaries for primary care visits up to the applicable Medicare cost sharing amount | ……… | ……… | −10 | −10 | −10 | −10 | −10 | −10 | −10 | ……… | −10 | −40 | −70 |
| Allow CMS to assign beneficiaries to Federally Qualified Health Centers and Rural Health Centers participating in the Medicare Shared Savings Program | ……… | ……… | ……… | ……… | −10 | −10 | −10 | −10 | −10 | −10 | −20 | −20 | −80 |
| Expand basis for beneficiary assignment for Accountable Care Organizations to include Nurse Practitioners, Physician Assistants, and Clinical Nurse Specialists | ……… | ……… | ……… | −10 | −10 | −10 | −20 | −20 | −20 | −20 | −20 | −30 | −130 |
| Establish quality bonus payments for high-performing Part D plans | ……… | ……… | ……… | ……… | ……… | ……… | ……… | ……… | ……… | ……… | ……… | ……… | ……… |
| Implement bundled payment for post-acute care | ……… | ……… | ……… | ……… | ……… | −440 | −1,020 | −1,690 | −1,920 | −2,060 | −2,230 | −440 | −9,360 |
| Implement value-based purchasing for skilled nursing facilities (SNFs), home health agencies (HHAs), ambulatory surgical centers (ASCs), hospital outpatient departments (HOPDs), and community mental health centers (CMHCs) | ……… | ……… | ……… | ……… | ……… | ……… | ……… | ……… | ……… | ……… | ……… | ……… | ……… |
| Establish a hospital wide readmissions measure | ……… | ……… | ……… | ……… | ……… | ……… | ……… | ……… | ……… | ……… | ……… | ……… | ……… |
| Extend accountability for hospital-acquired conditions | ……… | ……… | ……… | ……… | ……… | ……… | ……… | ……… | ……… | ……… | ……… | ……… | ……… |

## Table S-8. MANDATORY AND RECEIPT PROPOSALS—Continued
(Deficit increases (+) or decreases (−) in millions of dollars)

|  | 2015 | 2016 | 2017 | 2018 | 2019 | 2020 | 2021 | 2022 | 2023 | 2024 | 2025 | Totals 2016-2020 | Totals 2016-2025 |
|---|---|---|---|---|---|---|---|---|---|---|---|---|---|
| **Improve beneficiary access:** | | | | | | | | | | | | | |
| Eliminate the 190-day lifetime limit on inpatient psychiatric facility services | ......... | 60 | 70 | 70 | 80 | 80 | 80 | 80 | 100 | 100 | 110 | 360 | 830 |
| Expand coverage of dialysis services for beneficiaries with acute kidney injury | ......... | −20 | −20 | −20 | −20 | −20 | −20 | −20 | −20 | −30 | −30 | −100 | −220 |
| **Bad debts:** | | | | | | | | | | | | | |
| Reduce Medicare coverage of bad debts | ......... | −370 | −1,260 | −2,430 | −3,100 | −3,360 | −3,590 | −3,840 | −4,110 | −4,380 | −4,680 | −10,520 | −31,120 |
| **Graduate medical education:** | | | | | | | | | | | | | |
| Better align graduate medical education payments with patient care costs | ......... | −1,010 | −1,280 | −1,370 | −1,460 | −1,560 | −1,680 | −1,800 | −1,930 | −2,050 | −2,180 | −6,680 | −16,320 |
| **Better align payments to rural providers with the cost of health care:** | | | | | | | | | | | | | |
| Reduce Critical Access Hospital (CAH) payments from 101% of reasonable costs to 100% of reasonable costs | ......... | −110 | −130 | −150 | −150 | −170 | −180 | −190 | −210 | −230 | −240 | −710 | −1,760 |
| Prohibit CAH designation for facilities that are less than 10 miles from the nearest hospital | ......... | −60 | −60 | −70 | −70 | −70 | −80 | −80 | −90 | −100 | −100 | −330 | −780 |
| **Cut waste, fraud, and improper payments in Medicare:** | | | | | | | | | | | | | |
| Reduce waste, fraud, and abuse in Medicare | ......... | 109 | 118 | 58 | −43 | −143 | −173 | −203 | −224 | −234 | −254 | 99 | −989 |
| **Drug rebates and additional Part D savings:** | | | | | | | | | | | | | |
| Align Medicare drug payment policies with Medicaid policies for low-income enrollees | ......... | ......... | −3,400 | −8,420 | −9,730 | −11,520 | −13,480 | −15,210 | −18,170 | −21,730 | −24,230 | −33,070 | −125,890 |
| Accelerate manufacturer discounts for brand drugs to provide relief to Medicare beneficiaries in the coverage gap | ......... | ......... | −50 | −350 | −620 | −1,230 | −1,380 | −1,540 | −1,470 | −1,370 | −1,610 | −2,250 | −9,620 |
| Suspend coverage and payment for questionable Part D prescriptions and incomplete clinical information | ......... | −60 | −60 | −70 | −60 | −70 | −80 | −80 | −90 | −100 | −110 | −320 | −780 |
| Establish authority for a program to prevent prescription drug abuse in Medicare Part D | ......... | ......... | ......... | −40 | −40 | −50 | −50 | −60 | ......... | ......... | ......... | ......... | ......... |
| Require mandatory reporting of other prescription drug coverage | ......... | −10 | −30 | −40 | −40 | −50 | −50 | −60 | −60 | −70 | −70 | −170 | −480 |
| Allow the Secretary to negotiate prices for biologics and high cost prescription drugs | ......... | ......... | ......... | ......... | ......... | ......... | ......... | ......... | ......... | ......... | ......... | ......... | ......... |
| **Encourage efficient post-acute care:** | | | | | | | | | | | | | |
| Adjust payment updates for certain post-acute care providers | ......... | −1,080 | −3,260 | −3,840 | −5,190 | −6,930 | −8,850 | −11,360 | −13,570 | −15,240 | −17,680 | −20,300 | −87,000 |

## Table S-8. MANDATORY AND RECEIPT PROPOSALS—Continued

(Deficit increases (+) or decreases (−) in millions of dollars)

|  | 2015 | 2016 | 2017 | 2018 | 2019 | 2020 | 2021 | 2022 | 2023 | 2024 | 2025 | Totals 2016-2020 | Totals 2016-2025 |
|---|---|---|---|---|---|---|---|---|---|---|---|---|---|
| Encourage appropriate use of inpatient rehabilitation hospitals (IRFs) by requiring that 75 percent of IRF patients require intensive rehabilitation services | ......... | −170 | −200 | −210 | −220 | −230 | −230 | −240 | −260 | −260 | −270 | −1,030 | −2,290 |
| Additional provider efficiencies: |  |  |  |  |  |  |  |  |  |  |  |  |  |
| Exclude certain services from the in-office ancillary services exception | ......... | ......... | −260 | −410 | −460 | −490 | −520 | −560 | −590 | −640 | −670 | −1,620 | −4,600 |
| Modify reimbursement of Part B drugs | ......... | −330 | −590 | −630 | −680 | −740 | −800 | −870 | −950 | −1,030 | −1,120 | −2,970 | −7,740 |
| Improve payment accuracy for Medicare Advantage (MA): |  |  |  |  |  |  |  |  |  |  |  |  |  |
| Increase the minimum MA coding intensity adjustment | ......... | ......... | −430 | −1,050 | −2,020 | −3,260 | −4,740 | −5,500 | −5,990 | −6,470 | −7,170 | −6,760 | −36,630 |
| Align employer group waiver plan payments with average MA plan bids | ......... | ......... | −480 | −660 | −680 | −720 | −740 | −760 | −770 | −800 | −860 | −2,540 | −6,470 |
| Other Medicare: |  |  |  |  |  |  |  |  |  |  |  |  |  |
| Clarify calculation of the late enrollment penalty for Medicare Part B premiums | ......... | ......... | ......... | ......... | ......... | ......... | ......... | ......... | ......... | ......... | ......... | ......... | ......... |
| Clarify the Medicare Fraction in the Medicare DSH statute | ......... | ......... | ......... | ......... | ......... | ......... | ......... | ......... | ......... | ......... | ......... | ......... | ......... |
| Strengthen the Independent Payment Advisory Board (IPAB) to reduce long-term drivers of Medicare cost growth | ......... | ......... | ......... | ......... | ......... | ......... | −995 | −1,402 | −4,661 | −6,080 | −9,481 | ......... | −22,619 |
| Total, Medicare providers | ......... | −3,051 | −11,772 | −20,832 | −26,643 | −34,253 | −42,578 | −49,855 | −60,005 | −68,334 | −79,065 | −96,551 | −396,388 |
| Medicare structural reforms: |  |  |  |  |  |  |  |  |  |  |  |  |  |
| Increase income-related premiums under Medicare Parts B and D | ......... | ......... | ......... | −1,180 | −2,130 | −3,050 | −4,100 | −5,400 | −6,880 | −6,820 | −3,310 | −29,560 |
| Modify the Part B deductible for new beneficiaries | ......... | ......... | ......... | ......... | −60 | −70 | −300 | −420 | −900 | −1,050 | −1,130 | −130 | −3,930 |
| Introduce a Part B premium surcharge for new beneficiaries who purchase near first-dollar Medigap coverage | ......... | ......... | ......... | ......... | −90 | −130 | −130 | −140 | −150 | −150 | −160 | −220 | −950 |
| Introduce home health co-payments for new beneficiaries | ......... | ......... | ......... | ......... | −20 | −70 | −110 | −170 | −230 | −290 | −360 | −90 | −1,250 |
| Encourage the use of generic drugs by low-income beneficiaries | ......... | ......... | −530 | −760 | −820 | −900 | −960 | −1,040 | −1,130 | −1,210 | −1,300 | −3,010 | −8,650 |
| Total, Medicare structural reforms | ......... | ......... | −530 | −760 | −2,170 | −3,300 | −4,550 | −5,870 | −7,810 | −9,580 | −9,770 | −6,760 | −44,340 |
| Interactions | ......... | 38 | 84 | 1,555 | 4,291 | 5,374 | 7,124 | 6,974 | 12,379 | 10,444 | 15,260 | 11,342 | 63,523 |
| Medicaid and other: |  |  |  |  |  |  |  |  |  |  |  |  |  |
| Medicaid: |  |  |  |  |  |  |  |  |  |  |  |  |  |
| Limit Medicaid reimbursement of durable medical equipment based on Medicare rates | ......... | −310 | −330 | −350 | −370 | −390 | −410 | −430 | −455 | −475 | −500 | −1,750 | −4,020 |

## Table S–8. MANDATORY AND RECEIPT PROPOSALS—Continued
(Deficit increases (+) or decreases (–) in millions of dollars)

| | 2015 | 2016 | 2017 | 2018 | 2019 | 2020 | 2021 | 2022 | 2023 | 2024 | 2025 | Totals 2016-2020 | Totals 2016-2025 |
|---|---|---|---|---|---|---|---|---|---|---|---|---|---|
| Reduce waste, fraud, and abuse in Medicaid | ......... | –63 | –94 | –125 | –126 | –125 | –121 | –121 | –116 | –117 | –117 | –533 | –1,125 |
| Strengthen the Medicaid Drug Rebate program | ......... | –247 | –467 | –482 | –502 | –527 | –567 | –607 | –662 | –732 | –822 | –2,223 | –5,610 |
| Exclude brand-name and authorized generic drug prices from Medicaid Federal upper limit (FUL) | ......... | –30 | –60 | –90 | –90 | –90 | –90 | –90 | –90 | –90 | –90 | –360 | –810 |
| Increase access to and transparency of Medicaid drug pricing data | ......... | 6 | 6 | 6 | 6 | 6 | ......... | ......... | ......... | ......... | ......... | 30 | 30 |
| Create demonstration to address over-prescription of psychotropic medications for children in foster care | ......... | 114 | 211 | 211 | 218 | 225 | 83 | –14 | –11 | –9 | –6 | 979 | 1,022 |
| Allow States to develop age-specific health home programs | ......... | 200 | 210 | 90 | 90 | 90 | 80 | 90 | 90 | 90 | 90 | 680 | 1,120 |
| Improve and extend Money Follows the Person Rebalancing Demonstration through 2020 | ......... | ......... | ......... | ......... | ......... | ......... | ......... | ......... | ......... | ......... | ......... | ......... | ......... |
| Provide home and community-based services (HCBS) to children eligible for psychiatric residential treatment facilities | ......... | ......... | 73 | 151 | 157 | 165 | 172 | 180 | 188 | 197 | 206 | 546 | 1,489 |
| Allow full Medicaid benefits for individuals in a home and community-based services (HCBS) State plan option | ......... | ......... | 1 | 1 | 1 | 1 | 1 | 1 | 1 | 1 | 1 | 4 | 10 |
| Expand eligibility for the 1915(i) HCBS State plan option | ......... | 7 | 15 | 23 | 32 | 42 | 44 | 46 | 49 | 51 | 53 | 119 | 362 |
| Expand eligibility under the Community First Choice option | ......... | 238 | 255 | 296 | 319 | 343 | 368 | 395 | 424 | 455 | 488 | 1,451 | 3,581 |
| Pilot comprehensive long-term care State plan option | ......... | ......... | ......... | 763 | 795 | 829 | 865 | 903 | ......... | ......... | ......... | 2,388 | 4,156 |
| Permanently extend Express Lane Eligibility (ELE) for children | ......... | ......... | ......... | 30 | 55 | 60 | 75 | 90 | 105 | 115 | 130 | 145 | 660 |
| Create State option to provide 12-month continuous Medicaid eligibility for adults [3] | ......... | 317 | 433 | 932 | 737 | 709 | 687 | 759 | 830 | 788 | 942 | 3,128 | 7,134 |
| Allow pregnant women choice of Medicaid eligibility category | ......... | ......... | ......... | ......... | ......... | ......... | ......... | ......... | ......... | ......... | ......... | ......... | ......... |
| Expand State flexibility to provide benchmark benefit packages | ......... | ......... | ......... | ......... | ......... | ......... | ......... | ......... | ......... | ......... | ......... | ......... | ......... |
| Require full coverage of preventive health and tobacco cessation services for adults in traditional Medicaid | ......... | 94 | 91 | 86 | 81 | 76 | 71 | 67 | 64 | 62 | 61 | 428 | 754 |
| Require coverage of EPSDT for children in inpatient psychiatric treatment facilities | ......... | 35 | 35 | 40 | 40 | 45 | 45 | 50 | 50 | 55 | 60 | 195 | 455 |
| Total, Medicaid | ......... | 362 | 379 | 1,582 | 1,444 | 1,459 | 1,304 | 1,320 | 1,467 | 392 | 498 | 5,227 | 9,208 |

## Table S-8. MANDATORY AND RECEIPT PROPOSALS—Continued
(Deficit increases (+) or decreases (–) in millions of dollars)

| | 2015 | 2016 | 2017 | 2018 | 2019 | 2020 | 2021 | 2022 | 2023 | 2024 | 2025 | Totals 2016-2020 | Totals 2016-2025 |
|---|---|---|---|---|---|---|---|---|---|---|---|---|---|
| **Medicare - Medicaid enrollees:** | | | | | | | | | | | | | |
| Ensure retroactive Part D coverage of newly-eligible low-income beneficiaries | ...... | ...... | ...... | ...... | ...... | ...... | ...... | ...... | ...... | ...... | 10 | ...... | 10 |
| Establish integrated appeals process for Medicare-Medicaid enrollees | ...... | ...... | ...... | ...... | ...... | ...... | ...... | ...... | ...... | ...... | ...... | ...... | ...... |
| Create pilot to expand PACE eligibilty to individuals between ages 21 and 55 | ...... | ...... | ...... | ...... | ...... | ...... | ...... | ...... | ...... | ...... | ...... | ...... | ...... |
| Allow for Federal/State coordinated review of Duals Special Need Plan marketing materials | ...... | ...... | ...... | ...... | ...... | ...... | ...... | ...... | ...... | ...... | ...... | ...... | ...... |
| Total, Medicare - Medicaid enrollees | ...... | ...... | ...... | ...... | ...... | ...... | ...... | ...... | ...... | ...... | 10 | ...... | 10 |
| **Pharmaceutical savings:** | | | | | | | | | | | | | |
| Prohibit brand and generic drug manufacturers from delaying the availability of new generic drugs and biologics | ...... | –850 | –900 | –970 | –1,070 | –1,150 | –1,230 | –1,340 | –1,440 | –1,540 | –1,650 | –4,940 | –12,140 |
| Modify length of exclusivity to facilitate faster development of generic biologics | ...... | ...... | 30 | –70 | –340 | –520 | –600 | –650 | –740 | –760 | –770 | –900 | –4,420 |
| Total, pharmaceutical savings | ...... | –850 | –870 | –1,040 | –1,410 | –1,670 | –1,830 | –1,990 | –2,180 | –2,300 | –2,420 | –5,840 | –16,560 |
| Allow CMS to reinvest civil monetary penalties recovered from home health agencies | ...... | 1 | 1 | 1 | 1 | 1 | 1 | 1 | 1 | 1 | 1 | 5 | 10 |
| Allow CMS to assess a fee on Medicare providers for payments subject to the Federal Levy Program | ...... | ...... | ...... | ...... | ...... | ...... | ...... | ...... | ...... | ...... | ...... | ...... | ...... |
| Reauthorize Special Diabetes Program | ...... | ...... | ...... | 180 | 86 | 26 | 4 | 4 | ...... | ...... | ...... | 292 | 300 |
| Extend Health Centers | ...... | ...... | ...... | 1,350 | 1,188 | 81 | 54 | 27 | ...... | ...... | ...... | 2,619 | 2,700 |
| Total, Medicaid and other | ...... | –487 | –490 | 2,073 | 1,309 | –103 | –467 | –638 | –1,712 | –1,907 | –1,911 | 2,303 | –4,332 |
| **Medicare appeals:** | | | | | | | | | | | | | |
| Provide Office of Medicare Hearings and Appeals and Department Appeals Board authority to use RAC collections | ...... | 127 | 127 | 127 | 127 | 127 | 127 | 127 | 127 | 127 | 127 | 635 | 1,270 |
| Establish Medicare appeals refundable filing fee | ...... | ...... | ...... | ...... | ...... | ...... | ...... | ...... | ...... | ...... | ...... | ...... | ...... |
| Remand appeals to the redetermination level with the introduction of new evidence | ...... | ...... | ...... | ...... | ...... | ...... | ...... | ...... | ...... | ...... | ...... | ...... | ...... |
| Sample and consolidate similar claims for administrative efficiency | ...... | ...... | ...... | ...... | ...... | ...... | ...... | ...... | ...... | ...... | ...... | ...... | ...... |
| Increase minimum amount in controversy for Administrative Law Judge (ALJ) adjudication of claims to equal amount required for judicial review | ...... | ...... | ...... | ...... | ...... | ...... | ...... | ...... | ...... | ...... | ...... | ...... | ...... |

## Table S-8. MANDATORY AND RECEIPT PROPOSALS—Continued
(Deficit increases (+) or decreases (−) in millions of dollars)

| | 2015 | 2016 | 2017 | 2018 | 2019 | 2020 | 2021 | 2022 | 2023 | 2024 | 2025 | Totals 2016-2020 | Totals 2016-2025 |
|---|---|---|---|---|---|---|---|---|---|---|---|---|---|
| Establish magistrate adjudication for claims with amount in controversy below new ALJ amount in controversy threshold | ......... | ......... | ......... | ......... | ......... | ......... | ......... | ......... | ......... | ......... | ......... | ......... | ......... |
| Expedite procedures for claims with no material fact in dispute | ......... | ......... | ......... | ......... | ......... | ......... | ......... | ......... | ......... | ......... | ......... | ......... | ......... |
| Total, Medicare appeals | ......... | 127 | 127 | 127 | 127 | 127 | 127 | 127 | 127 | 127 | 127 | 635 | 1,270 |
| Health workforce investments: | | | | | | | | | | | | | |
| Create a competitive, value-based graduate medical education program | ......... | 40 | 165 | 280 | 398 | 465 | 487 | 515 | 538 | 565 | 587 | 1,348 | 4,040 |
| Extend the Medicaid primary care payment increase through CY 2016 and include additional providers | 5,580 | 7,450 | 1,860 | ......... | ......... | ......... | ......... | ......... | ......... | ......... | ......... | 9,310 | 9,310 |
| Invest in the National Health Service Corps | ......... | ......... | ......... | 262 | 487 | 508 | 256 | 37 | 16 | 5 | ......... | 1,257 | 1,571 |
| Total, health workforce investments | 5,580 | 7,490 | 2,025 | 542 | 885 | 973 | 743 | 552 | 554 | 570 | 587 | 11,915 | 14,921 |
| Provide CMS Program Management implementation funding | ......... | 25 | 300 | 75 | ......... | ......... | ......... | ......... | ......... | ......... | ......... | 400 | 400 |
| Provide CMS Program Management implementation funding for Physician Payment Reform | ......... | 10 | 30 | 35 | 15 | 5 | 5 | ......... | ......... | ......... | ......... | 95 | 100 |
| Total, HHS health savings [4] | 5,580 | 4,152 | −10,226 | −17,185 | −22,185 | −31,177 | −39,596 | −48,710 | −56,467 | −68,680 | −74,772 | −76,621 | −364,846 |
| Provide mandatory funding for Tribal contract support costs: | | | | | | | | | | | | | |
| PAYGO effects | ......... | ......... | 69 | 180 | 340 | ......... | ......... | ......... | ......... | ......... | ......... | 589 | 589 |
| Nonscoreable reclassification | ......... | ......... | 731 | 745 | 760 | 775 | 790 | 806 | 822 | 839 | 856 | 3,011 | 7,124 |
| Total, provide mandatory funding for tribal contract support costs | ......... | ......... | 800 | 925 | 1,100 | 775 | 790 | 806 | 822 | 839 | 856 | 3,600 | 7,713 |
| *Annual reduction to discretionary spending limits (non-add)* | ......... | ......... | *−731* | *−745* | *−760* | *−775* | *−790* | *−806* | *−822* | *−839* | *−856* | *−3,011* | *−7,124* |
| Extend CHIP funding through 2019 [3] | ......... | ......... | 205 | 1,884 | 3,607 | −670 | 145 | −39 | −41 | −43 | −38 | 5,026 | 5,171 |
| Promote Family Based Care | ......... | 78 | 43 | 19 | 1 | −19 | −29 | ......... | ......... | ......... | ......... | 122 | −68 |
| Provide enhanced funding for Tribes to implement Title IV-E programs | ......... | 27 | 30 | 28 | 5 | 4 | 4 | 4 | 4 | 4 | 4 | 94 | 114 |
| Establish Title IV-E funding for prevention and permanency services | ......... | 30 | 41 | 41 | 51 | 57 | 58 | 56 | 61 | 84 | 108 | 220 | 587 |
| Expand eligibility through age 23 for Chafee Foster Care Independence Program | ......... | ......... | ......... | ......... | ......... | ......... | ......... | ......... | ......... | ......... | ......... | ......... | ......... |
| Modernize child support and create a Child Support Research Fund | ......... | 150 | 169 | 269 | 290 | 360 | 396 | 438 | 436 | 433 | 305 | 1,238 | 3,246 |
| Reauthorize Family Connection Grants | ......... | ......... | 10 | 3 | 1 | ......... | ......... | ......... | ......... | ......... | ......... | 14 | 14 |
| Repurpose Temporary Assistance for Needy Families (TANF) Contingency Fund to support Pathways to Jobs initiative | ......... | ......... | ......... | ......... | ......... | ......... | ......... | ......... | ......... | ......... | ......... | ......... | ......... |
| Reauthorize the Personal Responsibility Education Program (PREP) | ......... | ......... | ......... | 2 | 24 | 57 | 72 | 51 | 18 | 1 | ......... | 83 | 225 |

## Table S–8. MANDATORY AND RECEIPT PROPOSALS—Continued
(Deficit increases (+) or decreases (–) in millions of dollars)

|  | 2015 | 2016 | 2017 | 2018 | 2019 | 2020 | 2021 | 2022 | 2023 | 2024 | 2025 | Totals 2016-2020 | Totals 2016-2025 |
|---|---|---|---|---|---|---|---|---|---|---|---|---|---|
| Reauthorize Health Profession and Opportunity Grants | ......... | ......... | ......... | 78 | 85 | 81 | 39 | 7 | ......... | ......... | ......... | 244 | 290 |
| Support demonstration to address overprescription of psychotropic drugs for children in foster care (Funding in Administration for Children and Families) | ......... | 1 | 20 | 55 | 71 | 52 | 28 | 16 | 6 | 1 | 1 | 199 | 251 |
| Expand access to high-quality, affordable care for young children | ......... | 2,969 | 3,889 | 4,632 | 5,599 | 6,639 | 7,709 | 9,205 | 10,787 | 12,476 | 14,422 | 23,728 | 78,327 |
| Establish LIHEAP Contingency Fund | ......... | 755 | 972 | 860 | 742 | 661 | 627 | 629 | 643 | 657 | 671 | 3,990 | 7,217 |
| Fund Upward Mobility Project | ......... | 300 | 300 | 300 | 300 | 300 | ......... | ......... | ......... | ......... | ......... | 1,500 | 1,500 |
| Provide researcher access to National Directory of New Hires (NDNH) | ......... | ......... | ......... | ......... | ......... | ......... | ......... | ......... | ......... | ......... | ......... | ......... | ......... |
| Extend and expand the Maternal, Infant, and Early Childhood Home Visiting Program | ......... | ......... | ......... | 40 | 210 | 770 | 1,005 | 1,395 | 1,555 | 1,895 | 2,055 | 1,020 | 8,925 |
| Total, Health and Human Services | 5,580 | 8,462 | –3,747 | –8,049 | –10,099 | –22,110 | –28,752 | –36,142 | –42,176 | –52,333 | –56,388 | –35,543 | –251,334 |
| **Homeland Security:** | | | | | | | | | | | | | |
| Reform the aviation passenger security user fee to more accurately reflect the costs of aviation security | ......... | –195 | –200 | –350 | –600 | –625 | –650 | –675 | –680 | –690 | –700 | –1,970 | –5,365 |
| Increase customs user fees | ......... | ......... | ......... | ......... | ......... | ......... | ......... | ......... | ......... | ......... | ......... | ......... | ......... |
| Increase immigration inspection user fees | ......... | ......... | ......... | ......... | ......... | ......... | ......... | ......... | ......... | ......... | ......... | ......... | ......... |
| Increase Express Consignment Courier fees | ......... | ......... | ......... | ......... | ......... | ......... | ......... | ......... | ......... | ......... | ......... | ......... | ......... |
| Total, Homeland Security | ......... | –195 | –200 | –350 | –600 | –625 | –650 | –675 | –680 | –690 | –700 | –1,970 | –5,365 |
| **Housing and Urban Development:** | | | | | | | | | | | | | |
| Provide funding for grants to reduce local barriers to housing development | ......... | 6 | 30 | 45 | 81 | 81 | 51 | 6 | ......... | ......... | ......... | 243 | 300 |
| **Interior:** | | | | | | | | | | | | | |
| Provide a fair return to taxpayers for the use of public resources: | | | | | | | | | | | | | |
| Enact Federal oil and gas management reforms | ......... | –50 | –120 | –125 | –150 | –170 | –185 | –200 | –215 | –225 | –240 | –615 | –1,680 |
| Reform hardrock mining on public lands | ......... | ......... | –2 | –4 | –5 | –5 | –6 | –6 | –11 | –17 | –24 | –16 | –80 |
| Repeal geothermal payments to counties | ......... | –4 | –4 | –4 | –5 | –5 | –5 | –5 | –5 | –5 | –5 | –22 | –47 |
| Enact offshore revenue reform | ......... | –34 | –26 | –367 | –375 | –376 | –378 | –380 | –385 | –393 | –415 | –1,118 | –3,069 |
| Total, provide a fair return to taxpayers for the use of public resources | ......... | –54 | –126 | –500 | –535 | –556 | –574 | –591 | –616 | –640 | –684 | –1,771 | –4,876 |
| Ensure industry is held responsible for legacy pollution and risks to safety: | | | | | | | | | | | | | |
| Establish an abandoned mine lands (AML) hardrock reclamation fund [3] | ......... | –49 | –200 | –150 | –100 | –50 | ......... | ......... | ......... | ......... | ......... | –500 | –500 |
| Increase coal AML fee to pre-2006 levels [3] | ......... | ......... | –36 | –27 | –17 | –9 | –1 | 51 | 37 | 27 | 16 | –138 | –8 |
| Terminate AML payments to certified States | ......... | –34 | –26 | –35 | –36 | –30 | –27 | –25 | –10 | –1 | ......... | –161 | –224 |
| Fund AML reclamation and economic revitalization | ......... | 55 | 95 | 140 | 170 | 200 | 145 | 105 | 60 | 30 | ......... | 660 | 1,000 |

## Table S-8. MANDATORY AND RECEIPT PROPOSALS—Continued
(Deficit increases (+) or decreases (–) in millions of dollars)

|  | 2015 | 2016 | 2017 | 2018 | 2019 | 2020 | 2021 | 2022 | 2023 | 2024 | 2025 | Totals 2016-2020 | Totals 2016-2025 |
|---|---|---|---|---|---|---|---|---|---|---|---|---|---|
| Total, ensure industry is held responsible for legacy pollution and risks to safety | ......... | –28 | –167 | –72 | 17 | 111 | 117 | 131 | 87 | 56 | 16 | –139 | 268 |
| Conserve natural resources for future generations and provide recreation access to the public: |  |  |  |  |  |  |  |  |  |  |  |  |  |
| Establish dedicated funding for Land and Water Conservation Fund (LWCF) programs | ......... | 156 | 522 | 1,000 | 969 | 914 | 900 | 900 | 900 | 900 | 900 | 3,561 | 8,061 |
| Reauthorize the Federal Land Transaction Facilitation Act of 2000 (FLTFA) | ......... | –5 | –6 | –10 | –12 | –3 | ......... | ......... | ......... | ......... | ......... | –36 | –36 |
| Permanently reauthorize the Federal Lands Recreation Enhancement Act (FLREA) | ......... | ......... | ......... | ......... | ......... | ......... | ......... | ......... | ......... | ......... | ......... | ......... | ......... |
| Provide funding for a National Park Service Centennial Initiative | ......... | 95 | 360 | 500 | 405 | 140 | ......... | ......... | ......... | ......... | ......... | 1,500 | 1,500 |
| Total, conserve natural resources for future generations and provide recreation access to the public | ......... | 246 | 876 | 1,490 | 1,362 | 1,051 | 900 | 900 | 900 | 900 | 900 | 5,025 | 9,525 |
| Maintain commitments to communities and insular territories: |  |  |  |  |  |  |  |  |  |  |  |  |  |
| Provide mandatory funding for Tribal contract support costs: |  |  |  |  |  |  |  |  |  |  |  |  |  |
| PAYGO effects | ......... | ......... | 19 | 32 | 43 | 11 | ......... | ......... | ......... | ......... | ......... | 105 | 105 |
| Nonscoreable reclassification | ......... | ......... | 212 | 285 | 292 | 297 | 304 | 309 | 316 | 322 | 329 | 1,086 | 2,666 |
| Total, provide mandatory funding for tribal contract support costs | ......... | ......... | 231 | 317 | 335 | 308 | 304 | 309 | 316 | 322 | 329 | 1,191 | 2,771 |
| *Annual reduction to discretionary spending limits (non-add)* | ......... | ......... | –212 | –285 | –292 | –297 | –304 | –309 | –316 | –322 | –329 | –1,086 | –2,666 |
| Extend the Palau Compact of Free Association | ......... | 41 | 29 | 22 | 19 | 17 | 16 | 10 | 7 | 5 | ......... | 128 | 166 |
| Extend funding for Payments in Lieu of Taxes (PILT) | ......... | 452 | ......... | ......... | ......... | ......... | ......... | ......... | ......... | ......... | ......... | 452 | 452 |
| Improve coal miner retiree health and pension benefits | ......... | 363 | 375 | 380 | 385 | 389 | 389 | 404 | 408 | 411 | 411 | 1,892 | 3,915 |
| Total, maintain commitments to communities and insular territories | ......... | 856 | 635 | 719 | 739 | 714 | 709 | 723 | 731 | 738 | 740 | 3,663 | 7,304 |
| Total, Interior | ......... | 1,020 | 1,218 | 1,637 | 1,583 | 1,320 | 1,152 | 1,163 | 1,102 | 1,054 | 972 | 6,778 | 12,221 |
| **Labor:** |  |  |  |  |  |  |  |  |  |  |  |  |  |
| Unemployment Insurance reform:[5] |  |  |  |  |  |  |  |  |  |  |  |  |  |
| Strengthen Unemployment Insurance (UI) system solvency [3,6] | ......... | ......... | –3,889 | –4,263 | –4,207 | –4,643 | –4,877 | –5,154 | –5,143 | –5,110 | –5,663 | –17,002 | –42,949 |
| Improve UI Extended Benefits [3,6] | ......... | 2,722 | 2,417 | 2,997 | 4,210 | 5,268 | 6,076 | 5,462 | 5,556 | 6,010 | 5,692 | 17,614 | 46,410 |
| Modernize UI [3,6] | ......... | 2,253 | 1,647 | 455 | 394 | 97 | –35 | ......... | ......... | ......... | ......... | 4,845 | 4,810 |
| Reform the Federal Employees' Compensation Act | ......... | –19 | –9 | –14 | –21 | –29 | –34 | –41 | –49 | –56 | –64 | –92 | –336 |
| Improve Pension Benefit Guaranty Corporation (PBGC) solvency | ......... | 146 | 197 | –1,145 | –1,401 | –1,763 | –2,080 | –2,527 | –2,922 | –3,334 | –3,684 | –3,966 | –18,513 |

## Table S-8. MANDATORY AND RECEIPT PROPOSALS—Continued
(Deficit increases (+) or decreases (−) in millions of dollars)

| | 2015 | 2016 | 2017 | 2018 | 2019 | 2020 | 2021 | 2022 | 2023 | 2024 | 2025 | Totals 2016-2020 | Totals 2016-2025 |
|---|---|---|---|---|---|---|---|---|---|---|---|---|---|
| Extend the Trade Adjustment Assistance program [7] | ........ | 141 | 233 | 317 | 359 | 408 | 464 | 533 | 575 | 607 | 619 | 1,458 | 4,256 |
| Implement cap adjustments for UI program integrity [3,6] | ........ | −34 | −95 | −109 | −115 | −129 | −141 | −146 | −163 | −179 | −191 | −482 | −1,302 |
| *Outlays from discretionary cap adjustment (non-add)* | ........ | *30* | *35* | *40* | *45* | *50* | *55* | *60* | *65* | *70* | *75* | *200* | *525* |
| Improve UI program integrity (mandatory SIDES) [3,6] | ........ | −5 | −10 | −15 | −15 | −16 | −15 | −13 | −12 | −12 | −11 | −61 | −124 |
| Create Connecting for Opportunity program | ........ | 1,125 | 1,125 | 375 | 375 | ........ | ........ | ........ | ........ | ........ | ........ | 3,000 | 3,000 |
| Allow use of prisoner database for UI program integrity [3,6] | ........ | −3 | −6 | −7 | −8 | −6 | −6 | −5 | −5 | −5 | −4 | −30 | −55 |
| Expand Foreign Labor Certification fees | ........ | ........ | ........ | ........ | ........ | ........ | ........ | ........ | ........ | ........ | ........ | ........ | ........ |
| Create an Apprenticeship Training Fund | ........ | 500 | 500 | 500 | 500 | ........ | ........ | ........ | ........ | ........ | ........ | 2,000 | 2,000 |
| Provide High-Growth Sector Training and Credentialing Grants | ........ | 1,920 | 2,160 | 1,568 | 1,520 | 1,472 | 1,472 | 1,472 | 1,472 | 1,472 | 1,472 | 8,640 | 16,000 |
| Establish Paid Leave Partnership Initiative | ........ | 221 | 664 | 664 | 664 | ........ | ........ | ........ | ........ | ........ | ........ | 2,213 | 2,213 |
| Total, Labor | ........ | 8,967 | 4,934 | 1,322 | 2,254 | 659 | 823 | −418 | −691 | −608 | −1,834 | 18,137 | 15,410 |
| **Transportation:** | | | | | | | | | | | | | |
| Invest in surface transportation reauthorization | ........ | 4,914 | 11,561 | 15,229 | 16,883 | 17,986 | 18,978 | 15,686 | 9,553 | 6,009 | 4,121 | 66,573 | 120,920 |
| *Transfer to achieve trust fund solvency (non-add)* | ........ | *18,490* | *18,394* | *18,584* | *18,692* | *18,831* | *18,910* | ........ | ........ | ........ | ........ | *92,991* | *111,901* |
| **Treasury:** | | | | | | | | | | | | | |
| Establish a Pay for Success Incentive Fund | ........ | 29 | 21 | 10 | 24 | 40 | 56 | 46 | 42 | 24 | 8 | 124 | 300 |
| Authorize Treasury to locate and recover assets of the United States and to retain a portion of amounts collected to pay for the costs of recovery | ........ | −3 | −3 | −3 | −3 | −3 | −3 | −3 | −3 | −3 | −3 | −15 | −30 |
| Increase delinquent federal non-tax debt collections by authorizing administrative bank garnishment for non-tax debts | ........ | −32 | −32 | −32 | −32 | −32 | −32 | −32 | −32 | −32 | −32 | −160 | −320 |
| Allow offset of Federal income tax refunds to collect delinquent State income taxes for out-of-state residents | ........ | ........ | ........ | ........ | ........ | ........ | ........ | ........ | ........ | ........ | ........ | ........ | ........ |
| Reduce costs for States collecting delinquent income tax obligations | ........ | ........ | ........ | ........ | ........ | ........ | ........ | ........ | ........ | ........ | ........ | ........ | ........ |
| Provide authority to contact delinquent debtors via their cell phones | ........ | −12 | −12 | −12 | −12 | −12 | −12 | −12 | −12 | −12 | −12 | −60 | −120 |
| Reauthorize the State Small Business Credit Initiative | ........ | 216 | 735 | 525 | 6 | 6 | 6 | 6 | 6 | ........ | ........ | 1,488 | 1,500 |
| Implement tax enforcement program integrity cap adjustment [3] | ........ | −432 | −1,451 | −2,926 | −4,476 | −6,095 | −7,481 | −8,475 | −9,077 | −9,503 | −9,819 | −15,380 | −59,735 |
| *Outlays from discretionary cap adjustment (non-add)* | ........ | *667* | *1,039* | *1,403* | *1,781* | *2,170* | *2,232* | *2,276* | *2,329* | *2,382* | *2,437* | *7,060* | *18,716* |
| Total, Treasury | ........ | −234 | −742 | −2,438 | −4,493 | −6,096 | −7,466 | −8,470 | −9,082 | −9,526 | −9,858 | −14,003 | −58,405 |

## Table S-8. MANDATORY AND RECEIPT PROPOSALS—Continued
(Deficit increases (+) or decreases (−) in millions of dollars)

|  | 2015 | 2016 | 2017 | 2018 | 2019 | 2020 | 2021 | 2022 | 2023 | 2024 | 2025 | Totals 2016-2020 | Totals 2016-2025 |
|---|---|---|---|---|---|---|---|---|---|---|---|---|---|
| **Veterans Affairs:** | | | | | | | | | | | | | |
| Extend round-down of cost of living adjustments (compensation) | ...... | –36 | –74 | –121 | –159 | –192 | –204 | –214 | –225 | –234 | –244 | –582 | –1,703 |
| Extend round-down of cost of living adjustments (education) | ...... | ...... | –1 | –1 | –1 | –1 | –1 | –1 | –1 | –1 | –2 | –4 | –10 |
| Provide burial receptacles for certain new casketed gravesites | ...... | 4 | 1 | 7 | 2 | 1 | 4 | 4 | 5 | 4 | 5 | 15 | 30 |
| Improve housing grant program | ...... | 3 | 3 | 3 | 3 | 3 | 1 | 1 | 1 | 1 | 1 | 15 | 20 |
| Increase cap on vocational rehabilitation contract counseling | ...... | 1 | 1 | 1 | 1 | 1 | 1 | 1 | 1 | 1 | 1 | 5 | 10 |
| Extend supplemental service disabled veterans insurance coverage | ...... | ...... | ...... | ...... | ...... | 1 | ...... | ...... | 1 | 1 | 1 | 1 | 4 |
| Clarify evidentiary threshold at which VA is required to provide medical examination | ...... | –38 | –39 | –41 | –42 | –43 | –44 | –46 | –47 | –48 | –50 | –203 | –438 |
| Cap Post–9/11 GI Bill benefits for flight training | ...... | –26 | –27 | –28 | –30 | –31 | –33 | –35 | –36 | –39 | –41 | –142 | –326 |
| Expand eligibility for Montgomery GI Bill refund | ...... | 4 | 4 | 4 | 5 | 5 | 4 | 4 | 4 | 4 | 5 | 22 | 43 |
| Extend authorization of work-study activities | ...... | 1 | 1 | 1 | 1 | 1 | 1 | 1 | 2 | 2 | 2 | 5 | 12 |
| Pro-rate GI Bill benefit usage for certification tests | ...... | ...... | ...... | ...... | ...... | ...... | 1 | 1 | 1 | 1 | 1 | ...... | 5 |
| Modernize the definition of Automobile Adaptive Equipment (AAE) | ...... | –2 | –2 | –2 | –2 | –2 | –2 | –1 | –1 | –1 | –1 | –10 | –16 |
| Eliminate reductions of special monthly compensation for hospitalized veterans | ...... | ...... | ...... | 1 | 1 | 1 | ...... | 1 | 1 | 1 | 1 | 3 | 7 |
| Restore the eligibility of certain veterans for special aid and attendance allowance | ...... | 2 | 2 | 2 | 2 | 2 | 3 | 3 | 3 | 3 | 3 | 10 | 25 |
| Reissue VA benefit payments to all victims of fiduciary misuse | ...... | 2 | 2 | 2 | 2 | 2 | 2 | 2 | 2 | 2 | 2 | 10 | 20 |
| Total, Veterans Affairs | ...... | –85 | –129 | –172 | –217 | –252 | –267 | –279 | –290 | –307 | –319 | –855 | –2,317 |
| **Corps of Engineers:** | | | | | | | | | | | | | |
| Reform inland waterways funding [3] | ...... | –113 | –113 | –113 | –113 | –113 | –113 | –113 | –113 | –113 | –113 | –565 | –1,130 |
| **Environmental Protection Agency:** | | | | | | | | | | | | | |
| Eliminate statutory cap on pre-manufacture notice fee | ...... | –4 | –8 | –8 | –8 | –8 | –8 | –8 | –8 | –8 | –8 | –36 | –76 |
| Enact confidential business information management fee | ...... | ...... | –2 | –2 | ...... | ...... | ...... | ...... | ...... | ...... | ...... | –4 | –4 |
| Create Clean Power State Incentive Fund | ...... | ...... | 1,670 | 1,000 | 190 | 190 | 190 | 190 | 190 | 190 | 190 | 3,050 | 4,000 |
| Total, Environmental Protection Agency | ...... | –4 | 1,660 | 990 | 182 | 182 | 182 | 182 | 182 | 182 | 182 | 3,010 | 3,920 |
| **Executive Office of the President:** | | | | | | | | | | | | | |
| Promote Spectrum Relocation Fund flexibility [8] | ...... | 50 | –45 | –75 | –100 | –160 | –190 | –230 | –200 | –50 | ...... | –330 | –1,000 |
| **International Assistance Programs:** | | | | | | | | | | | | | |
| Mandatory effects of discretionary proposal to implement 2010 International Monetary Fund (IMF) agreement (non-scoreable) | ...... | –224 | ...... | ...... | ...... | ...... | ...... | ...... | ...... | ...... | ...... | –224 | –224 |

## Table S-8. MANDATORY AND RECEIPT PROPOSALS—Continued
(Deficit increases (+) or decreases (–) in millions of dollars)

|  | 2015 | 2016 | 2017 | 2018 | 2019 | 2020 | 2021 | 2022 | 2023 | 2024 | 2025 | Totals 2016-2020 | Totals 2016-2025 |
|---|---|---|---|---|---|---|---|---|---|---|---|---|---|
| **Other Defense—Civil Programs:** | | | | | | | | | | | | | |
| Increase TRICARE pharmacy copayments | ........ | –71 | –89 | –115 | –344 | –424 | –483 | –576 | –676 | –786 | –832 | –1,043 | –4,396 |
| Increase annual premiums for TRICARE-For-Life (TFL) enrollment | ........ | –3 | –15 | –43 | –83 | –111 | –141 | –173 | –206 | –240 | –276 | –255 | –1,291 |
| Increase TRICARE pharmacy copayments (accrual effects) | ........ | 315 | 328 | 343 | 361 | 382 | 403 | 426 | 451 | 476 | 505 | 1,729 | 3,990 |
| Increase annual premiums for TFL enrollment (accrual effects) | ........ | 83 | 85 | 87 | 89 | 92 | 97 | 103 | 109 | 115 | 123 | 436 | 983 |
| Total, Other Defense—Civil Programs | ........ | 324 | 309 | 272 | 23 | –61 | –124 | –220 | –322 | –435 | –480 | 867 | –714 |
| **Office of Personnel Management:** | | | | | | | | | | | | | |
| Streamline Federal Employee Health Benefit Plan (FEHBP) pharmacy benefit contracting | ........ | ........ | –59 | –124 | –143 | –153 | –164 | –176 | –187 | –200 | –213 | –479 | –1,419 |
| Provide FEHBP benefits to domestic partners | ........ | ........ | –7 | 6 | 18 | 29 | 40 | 54 | 69 | 85 | 103 | 46 | 397 |
| Expand FEHBP plan types | ........ | ........ | –1 | –3 | –4 | –7 | –9 | –10 | –14 | –19 | –21 | –15 | –88 |
| Adjust FEHBP premiums for wellness | ........ | ........ | 3 | –12 | –40 | –78 | –124 | –177 | –252 | –344 | –456 | –127 | –1,480 |
| Total, Office of Personnel Management | ........ | ........ | –64 | –133 | –169 | –209 | –257 | –309 | –384 | –478 | –587 | –575 | –2,590 |
| **Social Security Administration (SSA):** | | | | | | | | | | | | | |
| Provide dedicated, mandatory funding for program integrity: | | | | | | | | | | | | | |
| Administrative costs | ........ | ........ | 1,805 | 1,728 | 1,676 | 1,582 | 1,575 | 1,631 | 1,688 | 1,747 | 1,808 | 6,791 | 15,240 |
| Benefit savings | ........ | ........ | –238 | –2,003 | –3,163 | –3,902 | –4,532 | –5,394 | –5,714 | –5,950 | –6,796 | –9,306 | –37,692 |
| Total, provide dedicated, mandatory funding for program integrity | ........ | ........ | 1,567 | –275 | –1,487 | –2,320 | –2,957 | –3,763 | –4,026 | –4,203 | –4,988 | –2,515 | –22,452 |
| *Annual reduction to discretionary spending limits (non-add)* | ........ | ........ | *–273* | *–273* | *–273* | *–273* | *–273* | *–273* | *–273* | *–273* | *–273* | *–1,092* | *–2,457* |
| Allow SSA to use commercial databases to verify wages in SSI | ........ | ........ | ........ | ........ | –71 | –36 | –24 | –21 | –19 | –17 | –18 | –107 | –206 |
| Expand authority to require authorization to verify financial information for overpayment waiver requests [9] | ........ | –5 | –16 | –17 | –18 | –19 | –20 | –20 | –21 | –22 | –22 | –75 | –180 |
| Hold fraud facilitators liable for overpayments [9] | ........ | ........ | ........ | –1 | –1 | –1 | –1 | –1 | –1 | –1 | –1 | –3 | –8 |
| Allow Government-wide use of CBP entry/exit data to prevent improper payments | ........ | ........ | ........ | –2 | –7 | –14 | –22 | –33 | –40 | –43 | –52 | –23 | –213 |
| Clarify penalties and prohibitions for misleading Internet advertising | ........ | ........ | ........ | ........ | ........ | ........ | ........ | ........ | ........ | ........ | ........ | ........ | ........ |
| Allow Social Security benefits for same sex married couples | 1 | 5 | 8 | 9 | 11 | 13 | 13 | 14 | 14 | 14 | 14 | 46 | 115 |
| Lower electronic wage reporting threshold to five employees | ........ | ........ | ........ | ........ | ........ | ........ | ........ | ........ | ........ | ........ | ........ | ........ | ........ |
| Move from annual to quarterly wage reporting | ........ | 20 | 30 | 90 | –131 | –138 | –168 | –224 | –257 | –260 | –301 | –129 | –1,339 |
| Improve collection of pension information from States and localities | ........ | 18 | 28 | 24 | –351 | –776 | –1,047 | –1,142 | –1,085 | –1,075 | –1,054 | –1,057 | –6,460 |

## Table S–8. MANDATORY AND RECEIPT PROPOSALS—Continued
(Deficit increases (+) or decreases (–) in millions of dollars)

| | 2015 | 2016 | 2017 | 2018 | 2019 | 2020 | 2021 | 2022 | 2023 | 2024 | 2025 | Totals 2016-2020 | Totals 2016-2025 |
|---|---|---|---|---|---|---|---|---|---|---|---|---|---|
| Establish workers compensation information reporting | ......... | ......... | 5 | 5 | ......... | ......... | ......... | ......... | ......... | ......... | ......... | 10 | 10 |
| Extend SSI time limits for qualified refugees | ......... | ......... | 45 | 50 | ......... | ......... | ......... | ......... | ......... | ......... | ......... | 95 | 95 |
| Conform treatment of State and local government Earned Income Tax Credit (EITC) and Child Tax Credit (CTC) for SSI [10] | ......... | ......... | ......... | ......... | ......... | ......... | ......... | ......... | ......... | ......... | ......... | ......... | ......... |
| Terminate step-child benefits in the same month as step-parent [11] | ......... | ......... | ......... | ......... | ......... | ......... | ......... | ......... | ......... | ......... | ......... | ......... | ......... |
| Allow SSA to electronically certify certain RRB payments | ......... | ......... | ......... | ......... | ......... | ......... | ......... | ......... | ......... | ......... | ......... | ......... | ......... |
| Use the Death Master File to prevent Federal improper payments | ......... | ......... | ......... | ......... | ......... | ......... | ......... | ......... | ......... | ......... | ......... | ......... | ......... |
| Offset DI benefits for period of concurrent UI receipt [3,6] | ......... | ......... | –35 | –171 | –253 | –252 | –249 | –258 | –265 | –272 | –275 | –712 | –2,031 |
| Eliminate aggressive SSA claiming strategies | ......... | ......... | ......... | ......... | ......... | ......... | ......... | ......... | ......... | ......... | ......... | ......... | ......... |
| Reauthorize and expand demonstration authority for DI and SSI | ......... | ......... | 70 | 105 | 115 | 60 | ......... | ......... | ......... | ......... | ......... | 350 | 350 |
| Reallocate payroll taxes to address DI trust fund reserve depletion | ......... | ......... | ......... | ......... | ......... | ......... | ......... | ......... | ......... | ......... | ......... | ......... | ......... |
| Total, Social Security Administration (SSA) | 1 | 88 | 1,707 | –238 | –2,193 | –3,483 | –4,475 | –5,448 | –5,700 | –5,879 | –6,697 | –4,120 | –32,319 |
| **Other Independent Agencies:** | | | | | | | | | | | | | |
| Federal Communications Commission (FCC): | | | | | | | | | | | | | |
| Enact Spectrum License User Fee and allow the FCC to auction predominantly domestic satellite services | ......... | –225 | –325 | –425 | –550 | –550 | –550 | –550 | –550 | –550 | –550 | –2,075 | –4,825 |
| Postal Service: | | | | | | | | | | | | | |
| Enact Postal Service financial relief and reform: | | | | | | | | | | | | | |
| PAYGO effect | 769 | –1,234 | –2,182 | –2,353 | –4,226 | –4,399 | –4,472 | –4,495 | –4,419 | –4,344 | –4,318 | –14,394 | –36,442 |
| Non-scoreable effect | ......... | 11 | 2,823 | 5,379 | 4,202 | 4,399 | 4,472 | 4,495 | 4,419 | 4,344 | 4,318 | 16,814 | 38,862 |
| Total, enact Postal Service financial relief and reform | 769 | –1,223 | 641 | 3,026 | –24 | ......... | ......... | ......... | ......... | ......... | ......... | 2,420 | 2,420 |
| Railroad Retirement Board (RRB): | | | | | | | | | | | | | |
| Amend Railroad Retirement Act and the Railroad Unemployment Insurance Act to include a felony charge for fraud | ......... | ......... | ......... | ......... | ......... | ......... | ......... | ......... | ......... | ......... | ......... | ......... | ......... |
| Promote RRB program integrity | ......... | 3 | 2 | 2 | 2 | 2 | 2 | 2 | 2 | 2 | 2 | 11 | 21 |
| Total, Railroad Retirement Board (RRB) | ......... | 3 | 2 | 2 | 2 | 2 | 2 | 2 | 2 | 2 | 2 | 11 | 21 |
| National Infrastructure Bank: | | | | | | | | | | | | | |
| Create infrastructure bank | ......... | 33 | 153 | 373 | 595 | 831 | 1,058 | 1,158 | 1,233 | 1,207 | 1,062 | 1,985 | 7,703 |
| Civilian Property Realignment Board: | | | | | | | | | | | | | |
| Dispose of unneeded real property | ......... | –87 | –63 | –136 | –495 | –65 | –50 | –60 | –60 | –40 | –40 | –846 | –1,096 |
| Total, Other Independent Agencies | 769 | –1,499 | 408 | 2,840 | –472 | 218 | 460 | 550 | 625 | 619 | 474 | 1,495 | 4,223 |

## Table S–8. MANDATORY AND RECEIPT PROPOSALS—Continued
(Deficit increases (+) or decreases (–) in millions of dollars)

|  | 2015 | 2016 | 2017 | 2018 | 2019 | 2020 | 2021 | 2022 | 2023 | 2024 | 2025 | Totals 2016-2020 | Totals 2016-2025 |
|---|---|---|---|---|---|---|---|---|---|---|---|---|---|
| **Multi-Agency:** | | | | | | | | | | | | | |
| Enact immigration reform [3] | ......... | 4,000 | 3,000 | –5,000 | –10,000 | –20,000 | –20,000 | –25,000 | –29,000 | –34,000 | –34,000 | –28,000 | –170,000 |
| Establish a consolidated TRICARE program (mandatory effects in Coast Guard, Public Health Service, and National Oceanic and Atmospheric Administration) | ......... | 1 | –7 | –14 | –14 | –15 | –17 | –17 | –19 | –20 | –21 | –49 | –143 |
| Modernize Military Retirement: | | | | | | | | | | | | | |
| PAYGO effect [3] | ......... | ......... | ......... | 157 | 182 | 225 | 253 | 269 | 282 | 298 | 309 | 564 | 1,975 |
| Non-scoreable effect | ......... | ......... | ......... | 1,296 | 1,491 | 1,726 | 1,975 | 2,203 | 2,423 | 2,646 | 2,870 | 4,513 | 16,630 |
| Sunset Montgomery GI Bill and Chapter 1607 Reserve Education Assistance Programs (REAP): | | | | | | | | | | | | | |
| PAYGO effect | ......... | 131 | 96 | 65 | 48 | 90 | 75 | 61 | 57 | 49 | 46 | 430 | 718 |
| Non-scoreable effect | ......... | 18 | 9 | 9 | 9 | 9 | 9 | 9 | 9 | 9 | 9 | 54 | 99 |
| Auction or assign via fee 1675–1680 megahertz | ......... | ......... | –150 | –150 | ......... | ......... | ......... | ......... | ......... | ......... | ......... | –300 | –300 |
| Reconcile OPM/SSA retroactive disability payments | 6 | ......... | ......... | –48 | –48 | –48 | –48 | –48 | –48 | –48 | –48 | –144 | –384 |
| Index the $750 benefit protection threshold for inflation | ......... | 1,890 | 9 | 14 | 21 | 27 | 33 | 40 | 46 | 53 | 60 | 1,961 | 2,193 |
| Establish hold harmless for Federal poverty guidelines | ......... | –38,608 | –2,684 | 41,292 | ......... | ......... | ......... | ......... | ......... | ......... | ......... | ......... | ......... |
| Adjust payment timing | ......... | ......... | ......... | ......... | ......... | ......... | ......... | –57,173 | –4,420 | 61,593 | ......... | ......... | ......... |
| Mandatory effects of proposal to authorize additional Afghan SIVs | ......... | ......... | 21 | 20 | 18 | 19 | 18 | 17 | 15 | 16 | 16 | 78 | 160 |
| Total, Multi-Agency | 6 | –32,568 | 294 | 37,641 | –8,293 | –17,967 | –17,702 | –79,639 | –30,655 | 30,596 | –30,759 | –20,893 | –149,052 |
| **Total, mandatory initiatives and savings** | 6,356 | –13,750 | 16,719 | 52,043 | 2,459 | –18,094 | –21,998 | –94,865 | –55,809 | –8,212 | –74,806 | 39,376 | –216,314 |
| **Tax proposals:** | | | | | | | | | | | | | |
| **Middle-class and pro-work tax reforms:** | | | | | | | | | | | | | |
| Reform child care tax incentives [12] | ......... | 2,024 | 4,110 | 4,276 | 4,491 | 4,730 | 4,948 | 5,163 | 5,374 | 5,583 | 6,005 | 19,631 | 46,704 |
| Simplify and better target tax benefits for education [12] | ......... | 6 | 1,867 | 4,777 | 4,726 | 5,127 | 5,315 | 5,871 | 5,835 | 6,475 | 6,527 | 16,503 | 46,526 |
| Provide for automatic enrollment in IRAs, including a small employer tax credit, increase the tax credit for small employer plan start-up costs, and provide an additional tax credit for small employer plans newly offering auto-enrollment [12] | ......... | ......... | 987 | 1,548 | 1,620 | 1,627 | 1,683 | 1,845 | 1,979 | 2,177 | 2,393 | 5,782 | 15,859 |
| Expand penalty-free withdrawals for long-term unemployed | ......... | 156 | 226 | 231 | 235 | 240 | 245 | 250 | 255 | 260 | 265 | 1,088 | 2,363 |
| Require retirement plans to allow long-term part-time workers to participate | ......... | 39 | 55 | 54 | 53 | 52 | 50 | 47 | 44 | 40 | 34 | 253 | 468 |
| Facilitate annuity portability | ......... | ......... | ......... | ......... | –3 | –17 | –35 | –56 | –84 | –118 | –159 | –8 | –460 |
| Simplify minimum required distribution rules | ......... | 5 | 5 | 2 | ......... | ......... | ......... | ......... | ......... | ......... | ......... | ......... | ......... |

SUMMARY TABLES

## Table S–8. MANDATORY AND RECEIPT PROPOSALS—Continued
(Deficit increases (+) or decreases (–) in millions of dollars)

|  | 2015 | 2016 | 2017 | 2018 | 2019 | 2020 | 2021 | 2022 | 2023 | 2024 | 2025 | Totals 2016-2020 | Totals 2016-2025 |
|---|---|---|---|---|---|---|---|---|---|---|---|---|---|
| Allow all inherited plan and IRA balances to be rolled over within 60 days | ..... | ..... | ..... | ..... | ..... | ..... | ..... | ..... | ..... | ..... | ..... | ..... | ..... |
| Expand EITC for workers without qualifying children [12] | ..... | 468 | 6,269 | 6,285 | 6,326 | 6,422 | 6,541 | 6,656 | 6,776 | 6,896 | 7,013 | 25,770 | 59,652 |
| Simplify the rules for claiming the EITC for workers without qualifying children [12] | ..... | 52 | 743 | 736 | 725 | 734 | 750 | 768 | 787 | 806 | 825 | 2,990 | 6,926 |
| Provide a second-earner tax credit [12] | ..... | 2,059 | 8,976 | 9,071 | 9,393 | 9,536 | 9,660 | 9,798 | 9,920 | 10,068 | 10,222 | 39,035 | 88,703 |
| Extend exclusion from income for cancellation of certain home mortgage debt | ..... | 5,841 | 3,309 | 829 | ..... | ..... | ..... | ..... | ..... | ..... | ..... | 9,979 | 9,979 |
| Total, middle-class and pro-work tax reforms | ..... | 10,650 | 26,547 | 27,809 | 27,566 | 28,451 | 29,157 | 30,342 | 30,886 | 32,187 | 33,125 | 121,023 | 276,720 |
| **Reforms to capital gains taxation, upper-income tax benefits, and the taxation of financial institutions:** | | | | | | | | | | | | | |
| Reduce the value of certain tax expenditures | ..... | –28,133 | –46,047 | –50,581 | –55,198 | –59,807 | –64,447 | –69,126 | –73,802 | –78,460 | –83,098 | –239,766 | –608,699 |
| Reform the taxation of capital income | ..... | –11,935 | –23,810 | –20,001 | –21,122 | –22,294 | –22,479 | –23,754 | –25,029 | –26,408 | –27,859 | –99,162 | –224,691 |
| Implement the Buffett Rule by imposing a new "Fair Share Tax" | ..... | –6,518 | 19 | –1,215 | –2,833 | –3,710 | –3,946 | –4,070 | –4,210 | –4,354 | –4,481 | –14,257 | –35,318 |
| Impose a financial fee | ..... | –5,590 | –10,980 | –10,881 | –11,112 | –11,370 | –11,631 | –11,899 | –12,173 | –12,453 | –12,739 | –49,933 | –110,828 |
| Total, reforms to capital gains taxation, upper-income tax benefits, and the taxation of financial institutions | ..... | –52,176 | –80,818 | –82,678 | –90,265 | –97,181 | –102,503 | –108,849 | –115,214 | –121,675 | –128,177 | –403,118 | –979,536 |
| **Loophole closers:** | | | | | | | | | | | | | |
| Require current inclusion in income of accrued market discount and limit the accrual amount for distressed debt | ..... | –4 | –12 | –20 | –27 | –34 | –41 | –49 | –58 | –68 | –78 | –97 | –391 |
| Require that the cost basis of stock that is a covered security must be determined using an average cost basis method | ..... | ..... | –67 | –204 | –349 | –504 | –596 | –619 | –645 | –673 | –702 | –1,124 | –4,359 |
| Tax carried (profits) interests as ordinary income | ..... | –1,297 | –2,428 | –2,437 | –2,332 | –2,227 | –2,146 | –1,754 | –1,334 | –1,098 | –1,015 | –10,721 | –18,068 |
| Require non-spouse beneficiaries of deceased IRA owners and retirement plan participants to take inherited distributions over no more than five years | ..... | –87 | –237 | –400 | –567 | –737 | –786 | –748 | –694 | –640 | –583 | –2,028 | –5,479 |
| Limit the total accrual of tax-favored retirement benefits | ..... | –1,418 | –2,044 | –2,170 | –2,223 | –2,455 | –2,631 | –2,783 | –3,074 | –3,157 | –3,322 | –10,310 | –25,277 |
| Conform SECA taxes for professional service businesses | ..... | –3,979 | –5,532 | –5,807 | –6,084 | –6,413 | –6,840 | –7,296 | –7,707 | –8,058 | –7,420 | –27,815 | –65,136 |
| Limit Roth conversions to pre-tax dollars | ..... | ..... | –14 | –23 | –24 | –38 | –49 | –50 | –51 | –67 | –79 | –99 | –395 |
| Eliminate deduction for dividends on stock of publicly-traded corporations held in ESOPs | ..... | –589 | –830 | –851 | –865 | –879 | –892 | –907 | –922 | –936 | –951 | –4,014 | –8,622 |
| Repeal exclusion of net unrealized appreciation in employer securities | ..... | –27 | –33 | –25 | –25 | –12 | –4 | –4 | 10 | 20 | 21 | –122 | –79 |
| Disallow the deduction for charitable contributions that are a prerequisite for purchasing tickets to college sporting events | ..... | –127 | –201 | –220 | –238 | –255 | –272 | –288 | –307 | –326 | –346 | –1,041 | –2,580 |
| Total, loophole closers | ..... | –7,528 | –11,398 | –12,157 | –12,734 | –13,554 | –14,257 | –14,498 | –14,782 | –15,003 | –14,475 | –57,371 | –130,386 |

## Table S-8. MANDATORY AND RECEIPT PROPOSALS—Continued
(Deficit increases (+) or decreases (−) in millions of dollars)

| | 2015 | 2016 | 2017 | 2018 | 2019 | 2020 | 2021 | 2022 | 2023 | 2024 | 2025 | Totals 2016-2020 | Totals 2016-2025 |
|---|---|---|---|---|---|---|---|---|---|---|---|---|---|
| **Incentives for job creation, clean energy, and manufacturing:** | | | | | | | | | | | | | |
| Designate Promise Zones [12] | ......... | 494 | 925 | 834 | 778 | 745 | 719 | 690 | 674 | 678 | 692 | 3,776 | 7,229 |
| Provide a tax credit for the production of advanced technology vehicles | ......... | 506 | 495 | 505 | 520 | 405 | 329 | 204 | −27 | −199 | −213 | 2,431 | 2,525 |
| Provide a tax credit for medium- and heavy-duty alternative-fuel commercial vehicles | ......... | 40 | 71 | 76 | 80 | 61 | 26 | 5 | ......... | ......... | ......... | 328 | 359 |
| Modify and extend the tax credit for the construction of energy-efficient new homes | ......... | 192 | 164 | 195 | 227 | 252 | 270 | 286 | 302 | 329 | 341 | 1,030 | 2,558 |
| Reduce excise taxes on LNG to bring into parity with diesel [13] | ......... | 4 | 6 | 7 | 7 | 8 | 8 | 8 | 9 | 9 | 10 | 32 | 76 |
| Enhance and modify the conservation easement deduction | ......... | 58 | 150 | 87 | −8 | −39 | −41 | −43 | −48 | −51 | −54 | 248 | 11 |
| Total, incentives for job creation, clean energy, and manufacturing | ......... | 1,294 | 1,811 | 1,704 | 1,604 | 1,432 | 1,311 | 1,150 | 910 | 766 | 776 | 7,845 | 12,758 |
| **Modify estate and gift tax provisions:** | | | | | | | | | | | | | |
| Restore the estate, gift, and generation-skipping transfer (GST) tax parameters in effect in 2009 | ......... | ......... | −14,540 | −15,844 | −17,221 | −18,629 | −20,325 | −22,102 | −24,107 | −26,444 | −28,996 | −66,234 | −188,208 |
| Require consistency in value for transfer and income tax purposes | ......... | ......... | −266 | −312 | −337 | −336 | −353 | −380 | −405 | −435 | −464 | −1,251 | −3,288 |
| Modify transfer tax rules for grantor retained annuity trusts (GRATs) and other grantor trusts | ......... | ......... | −1,049 | −1,246 | −1,412 | −1,566 | −1,885 | −2,277 | −2,622 | −3,049 | −3,251 | −5,273 | −18,357 |
| Limit duration of GST tax exemption | ......... | ......... | ......... | ......... | ......... | ......... | ......... | ......... | ......... | ......... | ......... | ......... | ......... |
| Extend the lien on estate tax deferrals where estate consists largely of interest in closely held business | ......... | ......... | ......... | −23 | −23 | −24 | −25 | −26 | −29 | −30 | −32 | −34 | −95 | −246 |
| Modify GST tax treatment of Health and Education Exclusion Trusts | ......... | ......... | 32 | 31 | 29 | 28 | 25 | 24 | 22 | 21 | 19 | 120 | 231 |
| Simplify gift tax exclusion for annual gifts | ......... | ......... | −78 | −173 | −245 | −320 | −389 | −428 | −517 | −617 | −724 | −816 | −3,491 |
| Expand applicability of definition of executor | ......... | ......... | ......... | ......... | ......... | ......... | ......... | ......... | ......... | ......... | ......... | ......... | ......... |
| Total, modify estate and gift tax provisions | ......... | ......... | −15,924 | −17,567 | −19,210 | −20,848 | −22,953 | −25,192 | −27,659 | −30,556 | −33,450 | −73,549 | −213,359 |
| **Other revenue raisers:** | | | | | | | | | | | | | |
| Increase and modify Oil Spill Liability Trust Fund financing [13] | ......... | −91 | −132 | −137 | −140 | −144 | −146 | −148 | −154 | −157 | −158 | −644 | −1,407 |
| Reinstate Superfund taxes [13] | ......... | −1,555 | −2,010 | −2,036 | −2,081 | −2,109 | −2,166 | −2,226 | −2,285 | −2,341 | −2,401 | −9,791 | −21,210 |
| Increase tobacco taxes and index for inflation [13] | ......... | −8,051 | −10,358 | −10,195 | −10,138 | −9,853 | −9,448 | −9,005 | −8,433 | −7,967 | −7,457 | −48,595 | −90,905 |
| Make unemployment insurance surtax permanent [6] | ......... | −1,111 | −1,531 | −1,554 | −1,576 | −1,597 | −1,621 | −1,644 | −1,669 | −1,696 | −1,703 | −7,369 | −15,702 |
| Total, other revenue raisers | ......... | −10,808 | −14,031 | −13,922 | −13,935 | −13,703 | −13,381 | −13,023 | −12,541 | −12,161 | −11,719 | −66,399 | −129,224 |
| **Reduce the tax gap and make reforms:** | | | | | | | | | | | | | |
| Expand information reporting: | | | | | | | | | | | | | |
| Improve information reporting for certain businesses and contractors | ......... | −16 | −39 | −65 | −89 | −93 | −97 | −101 | −106 | −110 | −116 | −302 | −832 |

## Table S–8. MANDATORY AND RECEIPT PROPOSALS—Continued
(Deficit increases (+) or decreases (–) in millions of dollars)

| | 2015 | 2016 | 2017 | 2018 | 2019 | 2020 | 2021 | 2022 | 2023 | 2024 | 2025 | Totals 2016-2020 | Totals 2016-2025 |
|---|---|---|---|---|---|---|---|---|---|---|---|---|---|
| Provide an exception to the limitation on disclosing tax return information to expand TIN matching beyond forms where payments are subject to backup withholding | ......... | ......... | ......... | ......... | ......... | ......... | ......... | ......... | ......... | ......... | ......... | ......... | ......... |
| Provide for reciprocal reporting of information in connection with the implementation of FATCA | ......... | ......... | ......... | ......... | ......... | ......... | ......... | ......... | ......... | ......... | ......... | ......... | ......... |
| Improve mortgage interest deduction reporting | ......... | –101 | –157 | –168 | –180 | –190 | –200 | –210 | –219 | –229 | –238 | –796 | –1,892 |
| Require Form W–2 reporting for employer contributions to defined contribution plans | ......... | ......... | ......... | ......... | ......... | ......... | ......... | ......... | ......... | ......... | ......... | ......... | ......... |
| Improve compliance by businesses: | | | | | | | | | | | | | |
| Increase certainty with respect to worker classification | ......... | –85 | –416 | –809 | –967 | –1,053 | –1,141 | –1,237 | –1,338 | –1,449 | –1,565 | –3,330 | –10,060 |
| Increase information sharing to administer excise taxes [13] | ......... | –4 | –9 | –13 | –14 | –16 | –16 | –17 | –18 | –19 | –20 | –56 | –146 |
| Provide authority to readily share information about beneficial ownership information of U.S. companies with law enforcement | ......... | ......... | –1 | –2 | –9 | –6 | –4 | –3 | –3 | –3 | –3 | –18 | –34 |
| Strengthen tax administration: | | | | | | | | | | | | | |
| Impose liability on shareholders to collect unpaid income taxes of applicable corporations | ......... | –390 | –448 | –450 | –457 | –466 | –480 | –498 | –523 | –552 | –587 | –2,211 | –4,851 |
| Streamline audit and adjustment procedures for large partnerships | ......... | –190 | –252 | –249 | –242 | –236 | –238 | –243 | –248 | –253 | –256 | –1,169 | –2,407 |
| Revise offer-in-compromise application rules | ......... | –1 | –1 | –2 | –2 | –2 | –2 | –2 | –2 | –2 | –2 | –8 | –18 |
| Expand IRS access to information in the National Directory of New Hires for tax administration purposes | ......... | ......... | ......... | ......... | ......... | ......... | ......... | ......... | ......... | ......... | ......... | ......... | ......... |
| Make repeated willful failure to file a tax return a felony | ......... | ......... | ......... | ......... | –1 | –1 | –1 | –1 | –2 | –2 | –2 | –2 | –10 |
| Facilitate tax compliance with local jurisdictions | ......... | –1 | –1 | –1 | –2 | –2 | –2 | –2 | –2 | –2 | –2 | –7 | –17 |
| Extend statute of limitations for assessment for overstated basis and State adjustments | ......... | ......... | ......... | –77 | –90 | –103 | –118 | –135 | –155 | –178 | –167 | –856 |
| Improve investigative disclosure statute | ......... | ......... | ......... | –1 | –1 | –1 | –1 | –1 | –2 | –2 | –2 | –2 | –10 |
| Allow the IRS to absorb credit and debit card processing fees for certain tax payments | ......... | –2 | –2 | –2 | –2 | –2 | –2 | –2 | –2 | –2 | –2 | –10 | –20 |
| Provide the IRS with greater flexibility to address correctable errors [12] | ......... | –29 | –62 | –64 | –65 | –67 | –69 | –69 | –71 | –73 | –75 | –287 | –644 |
| Enhance electronic filing of returns | ......... | ......... | ......... | –1 | –1 | –1 | –1 | –2 | –2 | –2 | –2 | –2 | –10 |
| Improve the whistleblower program | ......... | ......... | ......... | ......... | ......... | ......... | ......... | ......... | ......... | ......... | ......... | ......... | ......... |

## Table S-8. MANDATORY AND RECEIPT PROPOSALS—Continued
(Deficit increases (+) or decreases (−) in millions of dollars)

| | 2015 | 2016 | 2017 | 2018 | 2019 | 2020 | 2021 | 2022 | 2023 | 2024 | 2025 | Totals 2016-2020 | Totals 2016-2025 |
|---|---|---|---|---|---|---|---|---|---|---|---|---|---|
| Index all civil tax penalties for inflation | ......... | ......... | ......... | ......... | ......... | ......... | ......... | ......... | ......... | ......... | ......... | ......... | ......... |
| Extend IRS authority to require truncated Social Security Numbers on Form W–2 | ......... | ......... | ......... | ......... | ......... | ......... | ......... | ......... | ......... | ......... | ......... | ......... | ......... |
| Combat tax-related identity theft | ......... | ......... | ......... | ......... | ......... | ......... | ......... | ......... | ......... | ......... | ......... | ......... | ......... |
| Allow States to send notices of intent to offset Federal tax refunds to collect State tax obligations by regular first-class mail instead of certified mail | ......... | ......... | ......... | ......... | ......... | ......... | ......... | ......... | ......... | ......... | ......... | ......... | ......... |
| Rationalize tax return filing due dates so they are staggered [12] | ......... | −166 | −174 | −182 | −189 | −197 | −204 | −212 | −221 | −229 | −239 | −908 | −2,013 |
| Increase oversight and due diligence of tax return preparers: | | | | | | | | | | | | | |
| Extend paid preparer EITC due diligence requirements to the Child Tax Credit | ......... | ......... | ......... | ......... | ......... | ......... | ......... | ......... | ......... | ......... | ......... | ......... | ......... |
| Explicitly provide that the Department of the Treasury and IRS have authority to regulate all paid return preparers [12] | ......... | −15 | −31 | −35 | −38 | −43 | −46 | −50 | −54 | −58 | −63 | −162 | −433 |
| Increase the penalty applicable to paid tax preparers who engage in willful or reckless conduct | ......... | ......... | ......... | −1 | −1 | −1 | −1 | −1 | −1 | −1 | −1 | −3 | −8 |
| Enhance administrability of the appraiser penalty | ......... | ......... | ......... | ......... | ......... | ......... | ......... | ......... | ......... | ......... | ......... | ......... | ......... |
| Total, reduce the tax gap and make reforms | ......... | −1,000 | −1,593 | −2,043 | −2,337 | −2,467 | −2,608 | −2,768 | −2,949 | −3,143 | −3,353 | −9,440 | −24,261 |
| **Simplify the tax system:** | | | | | | | | | | | | | |
| Modify adoption credit to allow tribal determination of special needs | ......... | ......... | ......... | ......... | ......... | 1 | 1 | 1 | 1 | 1 | 1 | 1 | 6 |
| Repeal non-qualified preferred stock designation | ......... | −26 | −44 | −43 | −41 | −38 | −35 | −30 | −26 | −23 | −20 | −192 | −326 |
| Repeal preferential dividend rule for publicly traded and publicly offered REITs | ......... | ......... | ......... | ......... | ......... | ......... | ......... | ......... | ......... | ......... | ......... | ......... | ......... |
| Reform excise tax based on investment income of private foundations | ......... | ......... | 6 | 5 | 5 | 6 | 6 | 6 | 6 | 6 | 7 | 22 | 53 |
| Remove bonding requirements for certain taxpayers subject to Federal excise taxes on distilled spirits, wine, and beer | ......... | ......... | 2 | 10 | 18 | 28 | 38 | 46 | 58 | 68 | 76 | 58 | 344 |
| Simplify arbitrage investment restrictions | ......... | ......... | 1 | 3 | 5 | 7 | 10 | 12 | 17 | 20 | 22 | 16 | 97 |
| Simplify single-family housing mortgage bond targeting requirements | ......... | ......... | 1 | 3 | 5 | 7 | 9 | 11 | 13 | 15 | 17 | 16 | 81 |
| Streamline private business limits on governmental bonds | ......... | −11 | −16 | −19 | −21 | −23 | −25 | −27 | −29 | −30 | −32 | −90 | −233 |
| Repeal technical terminations of partnerships | ......... | 24 | 99 | 198 | 281 | 338 | 370 | 378 | 378 | 378 | 378 | 940 | 2,822 |
| Repeal anti-churning rules of section 197 | ......... | ......... | ......... | ......... | ......... | ......... | ......... | ......... | ......... | ......... | ......... | ......... | ......... |
| Repeal special estimated tax payment provision for certain insurance companies | ......... | 309 | 370 | 330 | 289 | 251 | 210 | 172 | 134 | 97 | 59 | 1,549 | 2,221 |
| Repeal the telephone excise tax [13] | | | | | | | | | | | | | |

SUMMARY TABLES 53

## Table S-8. MANDATORY AND RECEIPT PROPOSALS—Continued
(Deficit increases (+) or decreases (–) in millions of dollars)

| | 2015 | 2016 | 2017 | 2018 | 2019 | 2020 | 2021 | 2022 | 2023 | 2024 | 2025 | Totals 2016–2020 | Totals 2016–2025 |
|---|---|---|---|---|---|---|---|---|---|---|---|---|---|
| Increase the standard mileage rate for automobile use by volunteers | ........ | 16 | 49 | 51 | 53 | 54 | 55 | 56 | 58 | 59 | 61 | 223 | 512 |
| Consolidate contribution limitations for charitable deductions and extend the carryforward period for excess charitable contribution deduction amounts | ........ | 90 | 50 | 6 | 6 | 6 | 6 | 492 | 1,195 | 1,844 | 2,435 | 158 | 6,130 |
| Exclude from gross income subsidies from public utilities for purchase of water runoff management | ........ | ........ | ........ | ........ | ........ | ........ | ........ | ........ | ........ | ........ | ........ | ........ | ........ |
| Provide relief for certain accidental dual citizens | ........ | 60 | 103 | 55 | 23 | 24 | 25 | 26 | 28 | 29 | 30 | 265 | 403 |
| Total, simplify the tax system | ........ | 462 | 621 | 599 | 623 | 661 | 670 | 1,143 | 1,833 | 2,464 | 3,034 | 2,966 | 12,110 |
| **Trade initiatives:** | | | | | | | | | | | | | |
| Extend GSP [7,13] | ........ | 1,670 | 158 | ........ | ........ | ........ | ........ | ........ | ........ | ........ | ........ | 1,828 | 1,828 |
| Extend AGOA [7,13] | ........ | 155 | 157 | 167 | 176 | 185 | 195 | 206 | 216 | 227 | 239 | 840 | 1,923 |
| Total, trade initiatives | ........ | 1,825 | 315 | 167 | 176 | 185 | 195 | 206 | 216 | 227 | 239 | 2,668 | 3,751 |
| **Other initiatives:** | | | | | | | | | | | | | |
| Authorize the limited sharing of business tax return information to improve the accuracy of important measures of the economy | ........ | ........ | ........ | ........ | ........ | ........ | ........ | ........ | ........ | ........ | ........ | ........ | ........ |
| Eliminate certain reviews conducted by the U.S. Treasury Inspector General for Tax Administration | ........ | ........ | ........ | ........ | ........ | ........ | ........ | ........ | ........ | ........ | ........ | ........ | ........ |
| Modify indexing to prevent deflationary adjustments | ........ | ........ | ........ | ........ | ........ | ........ | ........ | ........ | ........ | ........ | ........ | ........ | ........ |
| Impose a 14-percent one-time tax on previously untaxed foreign income | ........ | –34,323 | –56,021 | –54,049 | –52,076 | –50,103 | –19,725 | ........ | ........ | ........ | ........ | –246,572 | –266,297 |
| Total, other initiatives | ........ | –34,323 | –56,021 | –54,049 | –52,076 | –50,103 | –19,725 | ........ | ........ | ........ | ........ | –246,572 | –266,297 |
| **Total, tax proposals** | ........ | –91,604 | –150,491 | –152,137 | –100,094 | –158,129 | –167,127 | –144,094 | –131,489 | –139,300 | –146,894 | –154,000 | –721,947 | –1,437,724 |
| **Grand total** | 6,356 | –105,354 | –133,772 | –158,129 | –185,221 | –166,092 | –226,354 | –195,109 | –155,106 | –228,806 | | –682,571 | –1,654,038 |
| **Addendum, Reserve for long-run revenue-neutral business tax reform:** | | | | | | | | | | | | | |
| **Reform the U.S. international tax system:** | | | | | | | | | | | | | |
| Restrict deductions for excessive interest of members of financial reporting groups | ........ | –2,566 | –4,533 | –4,987 | –5,485 | –6,034 | –6,637 | –7,301 | –8,031 | –8,834 | –9,718 | –23,605 | –64,126 |
| Provide tax incentives for locating jobs and business activity in the United States and remove tax deductions for shipping jobs overseas | ........ | 11 | 18 | 19 | 20 | 20 | 22 | 22 | 24 | 24 | 26 | 88 | 206 |
| Repeal delay in the implementation of worldwide interest allocation | ........ | 1,352 | 2,308 | 2,400 | 2,496 | 2,596 | 1,055 | ........ | ........ | ........ | ........ | 11,152 | 12,207 |
| Extend the exception under subpart F for active financing income | ........ | 4,081 | 7,006 | 7,356 | 7,724 | 8,110 | 8,516 | 8,942 | 9,389 | 9,858 | 10,351 | 34,277 | 81,333 |
| Extend the look-through treatment of payments between related CFCs | ........ | 488 | 838 | 880 | 924 | 971 | 1,019 | 1,070 | 1,124 | 1,180 | 1,239 | 4,101 | 9,733 |

## Table S-8. MANDATORY AND RECEIPT PROPOSALS—Continued
(Deficit increases (+) or decreases (−) in millions of dollars)

|  | 2015 | 2016 | 2017 | 2018 | 2019 | 2020 | 2021 | 2022 | 2023 | 2024 | 2025 | Totals 2016-2020 | Totals 2016-2025 |
|---|---|---|---|---|---|---|---|---|---|---|---|---|---|
| Impose a 19-percent minimum tax on foreign income | ......... | −11,395 | −18,884 | −19,045 | −19,392 | −19,758 | −20,314 | −20,901 | −21,763 | −22,540 | −23,503 | −88,474 | −197,495 |
| Impose a 14-percent one-time tax on previously untaxed foreign income [14] | ......... | ......... | ......... | ......... | ......... | ......... | ......... | ......... | ......... | ......... | ......... | ......... | −3,270 |
| Limit shifting of income through intangible property transfers | ......... | −88 | −177 | −214 | −252 | −293 | −336 | −385 | −441 | −505 | −579 | −1,024 | −3,270 |
| Disallow the deduction for excess non-taxed reinsurance premiums paid to affiliates | ......... | −341 | −607 | −657 | −697 | −732 | −771 | −815 | −849 | −882 | −918 | −3,034 | −7,269 |
| Modify tax rules for dual capacity taxpayers | ......... | −437 | −768 | −831 | −890 | −939 | −976 | −1,001 | −1,042 | −1,087 | −1,135 | −3,865 | −9,106 |
| Tax gain from the sale of a partnership interest on look-through basis | ......... | −183 | −253 | −266 | −279 | −293 | −308 | −323 | −339 | −356 | −374 | −1,274 | −2,974 |
| Modify sections 338(h)(16) and 902 to limit credits when non-double taxation exists | ......... | −54 | −95 | −102 | −105 | −105 | −105 | −105 | −105 | −105 | −106 | −461 | −987 |
| Close loopholes under subpart F | ......... | −1,449 | −2,519 | −2,699 | −2,890 | −3,094 | −3,312 | −3,543 | −3,789 | −4,051 | −4,330 | −12,651 | −31,676 |
| Restrict the use of hybrid arrangements that create stateless income | ......... | −116 | −201 | −215 | −230 | −246 | −264 | −283 | −304 | −326 | −350 | −1,008 | −2,535 |
| Limit the ability of domestic entities to expatriate | ......... | −113 | −311 | −530 | −769 | −1,031 | −1,317 | −1,630 | −1,970 | −2,340 | −2,743 | −2,754 | −12,754 |
| Total, reform the U.S. international tax system | ......... | −10,810 | −18,178 | −18,891 | −19,825 | −20,828 | −23,728 | −26,253 | −28,096 | −29,964 | −32,140 | −88,532 | −228,713 |
| **Simplification and tax relief for small business:** | | | | | | | | | | | | | |
| Expand and permanently extend increased expensing for small business | ......... | 19,923 | 9,902 | 8,175 | 7,133 | 6,343 | 5,916 | 5,775 | 5,695 | 5,758 | 5,906 | 51,476 | 80,526 |
| Expand simplified accounting for small business and establish a uniform definition of small business for accounting methods | ......... | 4,773 | 3,941 | 2,309 | 1,592 | 1,290 | 1,241 | 1,322 | 1,395 | 1,195 | 1,186 | 13,905 | 20,244 |
| Eliminate capital gains taxation on investments in small business stock | ......... | ......... | ......... | ......... | ......... | 237 | 820 | 1,476 | 2,094 | 2,709 | 3,321 | 237 | 10,657 |
| Increase the limitations for deductible new business expenditures and consolidate provisions for start-up and organizational expenditures | ......... | 387 | 481 | 475 | 468 | 464 | 462 | 460 | 456 | 452 | 447 | 2,275 | 4,552 |
| Expand and simplify the tax credit provided to qualified small employers for non-elective contributions to employee health insurance [12] | ......... | 63 | 184 | 176 | 152 | 137 | 98 | 111 | 75 | 58 | 25 | 712 | 1,079 |
| Total, simplification and tax relief for small business | ......... | 25,146 | 14,508 | 11,135 | 9,345 | 8,471 | 8,537 | 9,144 | 9,715 | 10,172 | 10,885 | 68,605 | 117,058 |
| **Incentives for manufacturing, research, and clean energy:** | | | | | | | | | | | | | |
| Enhance and make permanent research incentives | ......... | 10,927 | 9,151 | 10,198 | 11,211 | 12,198 | 13,173 | 14,141 | 15,105 | 16,072 | 17,045 | 53,685 | 129,221 |
| Extend and modify certain employment tax credits, including incentives for hiring veterans | ......... | 1,199 | 885 | 950 | 997 | 1,033 | 1,074 | 1,121 | 1,167 | 1,210 | 1,255 | 5,064 | 10,891 |
| Modify and permanently extend renewable electricity production tax credit and investment tax credit [12] | ......... | −618 | 836 | 2,286 | 2,738 | 3,248 | 3,647 | 3,970 | 4,413 | 6,133 | 10,131 | 8,490 | 36,784 |

# Table S-8. MANDATORY AND RECEIPT PROPOSALS—Continued

(Deficit increases (+) or decreases (–) in millions of dollars)

| | 2015 | 2016 | 2017 | 2018 | 2019 | 2020 | 2021 | 2022 | 2023 | 2024 | 2025 | Totals 2016-2020 | Totals 2016-2025 |
|---|---|---|---|---|---|---|---|---|---|---|---|---|---|
| Modify and permanently extend the deduction for energy-efficient commercial building property | ......... | 104 | 230 | 288 | 304 | 302 | 298 | 292 | 282 | 270 | 260 | 1,228 | 2,630 |
| Provide a carbon dioxide investment and sequestration tax credit [12] | ......... | ......... | ......... | 174 | 1,092 | 1,144 | 593 | 459 | 489 | 514 | 534 | 2,410 | 4,999 |
| Provide additional tax credits for investment in qualified property used in a qualifying advanced energy manufacturing project | ......... | ......... | 73 | 192 | 1,111 | 772 | 94 | –14 | –48 | –40 | –37 | 2,148 | 2,103 |
| Provide new Manufacturing Communities tax credit | ......... | 87 | 256 | 457 | 600 | 683 | 745 | 784 | 689 | 447 | 145 | 2,083 | 4,893 |
| Extend the tax credit for second generation biofuel production | ......... | 104 | 125 | 157 | 172 | 175 | 153 | 118 | 83 | 48 | 13 | 733 | 1,148 |
| Total, incentives for manufacturing, research, and clean energy | ......... | 11,803 | 11,556 | 14,702 | 18,225 | 19,555 | 19,777 | 20,871 | 22,180 | 24,654 | 29,346 | 75,841 | 192,669 |
| **Incentives to promote regional growth:** | | | | | | | | | | | | | |
| Modify and permanently extend the New Markets tax credit | ......... | 127 | 283 | 485 | 714 | 962 | 1,222 | 1,471 | 1,610 | 1,625 | 1,591 | 2,571 | 10,090 |
| Reform and expand the Low-Income Housing tax credit | ......... | 13 | 63 | 189 | 361 | 536 | 713 | 895 | 1,074 | 1,264 | 1,468 | 1,162 | 6,576 |
| Total, incentives to promote regional growth | ......... | 140 | 346 | 674 | 1,075 | 1,498 | 1,935 | 2,366 | 2,684 | 2,889 | 3,059 | 3,733 | 16,666 |
| **Incentives for investment in infrastructure:** | | | | | | | | | | | | | |
| Provide America Fast Forward Bonds and expand eligible uses [12] | ......... | 1 | 5 | 11 | 14 | 22 | 28 | 35 | 41 | 48 | 53 | 53 | 258 |
| Allow current refundings of State and local governmental bonds | ......... | 1 | 5 | 5 | 5 | 5 | 5 | 5 | 5 | 5 | 5 | 21 | 46 |
| Repeal the $150 million non-hospital bond limitation on all qualified 501(c)(3) bonds | ......... | ......... | 1 | 3 | 5 | 7 | 9 | 11 | 13 | 16 | 17 | 16 | 82 |
| Increase national limitation amount for qualified highway or surface freight transfer facility bonds | 6 | 34 | 60 | 93 | 125 | 153 | 167 | 163 | 136 | 96 | 55 | 465 | 1,082 |
| Provide a new category of qualified private activity bonds for infrastructure projects referred to as qualified public infrastructure bonds | ......... | 25 | 117 | 251 | 386 | 524 | 638 | 695 | 714 | 733 | 751 | 1,303 | 4,834 |
| Modify qualified private activity bonds for public education facilities | ......... | ......... | ......... | ......... | ......... | ......... | ......... | ......... | ......... | ......... | ......... | ......... | ......... |
| Modify treatment of banks investing in tax-exempt bonds | ......... | 5 | 38 | 131 | 225 | 317 | 405 | 493 | 574 | 630 | 616 | 716 | 3,434 |
| Repeal tax-exempt bond financing of professional sports facilities | ......... | –3 | –11 | –23 | –35 | –47 | –60 | –72 | –85 | –97 | –109 | –119 | –542 |
| Allow more flexible research arrangements for purposes of private business use limits | ......... | ......... | ......... | ......... | 1 | 1 | 1 | 3 | 3 | 3 | 4 | 2 | 16 |
| Modify tax-exempt bonds for Indian tribal governments | ......... | 4 | 12 | 12 | 12 | 12 | 12 | 12 | 12 | 12 | 12 | 52 | 112 |
| Exempt foreign pension funds from the application of FIRPTA | ......... | 120 | 206 | 216 | 227 | 238 | 250 | 263 | 276 | 290 | 304 | 1,007 | 2,390 |
| Total, incentives for investment in infrastructure | 6 | 187 | 433 | 699 | 965 | 1,232 | 1,455 | 1,608 | 1,689 | 1,736 | 1,708 | 3,516 | 11,712 |

## Table S-8. MANDATORY AND RECEIPT PROPOSALS—Continued
(Deficit increases (+) or decreases (−) in millions of dollars)

| | 2015 | 2016 | 2017 | 2018 | 2019 | 2020 | 2021 | 2022 | 2023 | 2024 | 2025 | Totals 2016-2020 | Totals 2016-2025 |
|---|---|---|---|---|---|---|---|---|---|---|---|---|---|
| **Eliminate fossil fuel tax preferences:** | | | | | | | | | | | | | |
| Treat publicly-traded partnerships for fossil fuels as C corporations | ...... | ...... | ...... | ...... | ...... | ...... | −243 | −339 | −358 | −377 | −395 | ...... | −1,712 |
| Eliminate oil and natural gas preferences: | | | | | | | | | | | | | |
| Repeal enhanced oil recovery credit [15] | ...... | ...... | ...... | ...... | ...... | ...... | ...... | ...... | ...... | ...... | ...... | ...... | ...... |
| Repeal credit for oil and natural gas produced from marginal wells [15] | ...... | ...... | ...... | ...... | ...... | ...... | ...... | ...... | ...... | ...... | ...... | ...... | ...... |
| Repeal expensing of intangible drilling costs | ...... | −2,381 | −3,349 | −2,477 | −1,964 | −1,649 | −1,304 | −890 | −729 | −758 | −789 | −11,820 | −16,290 |
| Repeal deduction for tertiary injectants | ...... | −7 | −10 | −10 | −10 | −10 | −10 | −10 | −10 | −10 | −10 | −47 | −97 |
| Repeal exception to passive loss limitations for working interests in oil and natural gas properties | ...... | −9 | −18 | −21 | −21 | −22 | −21 | −21 | −21 | −20 | −19 | −91 | −193 |
| Repeal percentage depletion for oil and natural gas wells | ...... | −877 | −1,418 | −1,327 | −1,243 | −1,136 | −996 | −861 | −733 | −604 | −468 | −6,001 | −9,663 |
| Repeal domestic manufacturing deduction for oil and natural gas production | ...... | −497 | −923 | −987 | −1,020 | −1,052 | −1,083 | −1,117 | −1,154 | −1,194 | −1,234 | −4,479 | −10,261 |
| Increase geological and geophysical amortization period for independent producers to seven years | ...... | −94 | −350 | −553 | −547 | −450 | −342 | −226 | −142 | −111 | −69 | −1,994 | −2,884 |
| Subtotal, eliminate oil and natural gas preferences | ...... | −3,865 | −6,068 | −5,375 | −4,805 | −4,319 | −3,756 | −3,125 | −2,789 | −2,697 | −2,589 | −24,432 | −39,388 |
| Eliminate coal preferences: | | | | | | | | | | | | | |
| Repeal expensing of exploration and development costs | ...... | −36 | −64 | −61 | −59 | −60 | −57 | −53 | −49 | −47 | −45 | −280 | −531 |
| Repeal percentage depletion for hard mineral fossil fuels | ...... | −176 | −287 | −275 | −266 | −234 | −203 | −187 | −172 | −154 | −140 | −1,238 | −2,094 |
| Repeal capital gains treatment for royalties | ...... | −14 | −27 | −28 | −30 | −31 | −32 | −34 | −35 | −36 | −38 | −130 | −305 |
| Repeal domestic manufacturing deduction for the production of coal and other hard mineral fossil fuels | ...... | −19 | −19 | −20 | −21 | −22 | −23 | −24 | −25 | −26 | −27 | −101 | −226 |
| Subtotal, eliminate coal preferences | ...... | −245 | −397 | −384 | −376 | −347 | −315 | −298 | −281 | −263 | −250 | −1,749 | −3,156 |
| Total, eliminate fossil fuel tax preferences | ...... | −4,110 | −6,465 | −5,759 | −5,181 | −4,666 | −4,314 | −3,762 | −3,428 | −3,337 | −3,234 | −26,181 | −44,256 |
| **Reform the treatment of financial and insurance industry products:** | | | | | | | | | | | | | |
| Require that derivative contracts be marked to market with resulting gain or loss treated as ordinary | ...... | −2,901 | −4,699 | −4,012 | −2,565 | −1,552 | −1,036 | −639 | −466 | −467 | −445 | −15,729 | −18,782 |
| Modify rules that apply to sales of life insurance contracts | ...... | −22 | −42 | −45 | −47 | −49 | −53 | −55 | −57 | −60 | −63 | −205 | −493 |
| Modify proration rules for life insurance company general and separate accounts | ...... | −426 | −730 | −759 | −776 | −782 | −805 | −842 | −868 | −892 | −919 | −3,473 | −7,799 |
| Expand pro rata interest expense disallowance for corporate-owned life insurance | ...... | −62 | −151 | −238 | −343 | −465 | −608 | −770 | −933 | −1,106 | −1,291 | −1,259 | −5,967 |

# Table S-8. MANDATORY AND RECEIPT PROPOSALS—Continued
(Deficit increases (+) or decreases (−) in millions of dollars)

|  | 2015 | 2016 | 2017 | 2018 | 2019 | 2020 | 2021 | 2022 | 2023 | 2024 | 2025 | Totals 2016–2020 | Totals 2016–2025 |
|---|---|---|---|---|---|---|---|---|---|---|---|---|---|
| Conform net operating loss (NOL) rules of life insurance companies to those of other corporations | ........ | −15 | −26 | −28 | −30 | −31 | −33 | −35 | −37 | −38 | −39 | −130 | −312 |
| Total, reform the treatment of financial and insurance industry products | ........ | −3,426 | −5,648 | −5,082 | −3,761 | −2,879 | −2,535 | −2,341 | −2,361 | −2,563 | −2,757 | −20,796 | −33,353 |
| **Other revenue changes and loophole closers:** | | | | | | | | | | | | | |
| Repeal LIFO method of accounting for inventories | ........ | −6,055 | −8,653 | −8,593 | −8,814 | −8,700 | −8,877 | −8,527 | −8,408 | −8,724 | −8,352 | −40,815 | −83,703 |
| Repeal lower-of-cost-or-market inventory accounting method | ........ | −717 | −1,440 | −1,450 | −1,453 | −847 | −248 | −258 | −270 | −281 | −293 | −5,907 | −7,257 |
| Modify like-kind exchange rules for real property and collectibles | ........ | −659 | −2,005 | −2,026 | −2,048 | −2,070 | −2,094 | −2,119 | −2,145 | −2,174 | −2,202 | −8,808 | −19,542 |
| Modify depreciation rules for purchases of general aviation passenger aircraft | ........ | −98 | −308 | −456 | −492 | −560 | −561 | −373 | −187 | −131 | −132 | −1,914 | −3,298 |
| Expand the definition of substantial built-in loss for purposes of partnership loss transfers | ........ | −6 | −7 | −7 | −7 | −7 | −8 | −8 | −10 | −10 | −10 | −34 | −80 |
| Extend partnership basis limitation rules to nondeductible expenditures | ........ | −69 | −97 | −102 | −105 | −108 | −110 | −112 | −114 | −116 | −118 | −481 | −1,051 |
| Limit the importation of losses under related party loss limitation rules | ........ | −63 | −87 | −92 | −95 | −97 | −99 | −100 | −102 | −104 | −106 | −434 | −945 |
| Deny deduction for punitive damages | ........ | −30 | −43 | −44 | −45 | −46 | −47 | −48 | −49 | −51 | −52 | −208 | −455 |
| Conform corporate ownership standards | ........ | −1 | −17 | −32 | −33 | −34 | −35 | −36 | −38 | −40 | −42 | −117 | −308 |
| Tax corporate distributions as dividends | ........ | −48 | −82 | −86 | −90 | −94 | −98 | −103 | −108 | −113 | −118 | −400 | −940 |
| Repeal FICA tip credit | ........ | −490 | −868 | −908 | −947 | −989 | −1,032 | −1,077 | −1,123 | −1,172 | −1,223 | −4,202 | −9,829 |
| Repeal the excise tax credit for distilled spirits with flavor and wine additives [13] | ........ | −85 | −112 | −112 | −112 | −112 | −112 | −112 | −112 | −112 | −112 | −533 | −1,093 |
| Total, other revenue changes and loophole closers | ........ | −8,321 | −13,719 | −13,908 | −14,241 | −13,664 | −13,321 | −12,873 | −12,666 | −13,028 | −12,760 | −63,853 | −128,501 |
| **Total, reserve for business tax reform that is revenue neutral in the long run** | 6 | 10,609 | −17,167 | −16,430 | −13,398 | −11,281 | −12,194 | −11,240 | −10,283 | −9,441 | −5,893 | −47,667 | −96,718 |

Note: For receipt effects, positive figures indicate lower receipts. For outlay effects, positive figures indicate higher outlays. For net costs, positive figures indicate higher deficits.

[1] For FY 2016, the additional funding is proposed as a CHIMP.

[2] In the summer of 2015, the President took action within his existing authority to implement eligibility expansions to income-based repayment plans proposed in the 2015 Budget. However, the Administration continues to seek to work with Congress to create a unified, simple, and better targeted PAYE program. The Budget would use the resulting savings presented in this table to help students and expand college access.

[3] The estimates for this proposal include effects on receipts. The receipt effects included in the totals above are as follows:

|  | 2015 | 2016 | 2017 | 2018 | 2019 | 2020 | 2021 | 2022 | 2023 | 2024 | 2025 | Totals 2016–2020 | Totals 2016–2025 |
|---|---|---|---|---|---|---|---|---|---|---|---|---|---|
| Reauthorize special assessment from domestic nuclear utilities | ........ | −204 | −208 | −213 | −218 | −223 | −228 | −233 | −238 | −244 | −249 | −1,066 | −2,258 |
| Create State option to provide 12-month continuous Medicaid eligibility for adults | ........ | ........ | −33 | −73 | −154 | −160 | −166 | −173 | −179 | −188 | −198 | −420 | −1,324 |
| Extend CHIP funding through 2019 | ........ | ........ | ........ | −129 | −564 | −538 | ........ | ........ | ........ | ........ | ........ | −1,231 | −1,231 |
| Establish an AML hardrock reclamation fund | ........ | ........ | −200 | −200 | −200 | −200 | −200 | −200 | −200 | −200 | −200 | −800 | −1,800 |

## Table S-8. MANDATORY AND RECEIPT PROPOSALS—Continued
(Deficit increases (+) or decreases (–) in millions of dollars)

|  | 2015 | 2016 | 2017 | 2018 | 2019 | 2020 | 2021 | 2022 | 2023 | 2024 | 2025 | Totals 2016–2020 | Totals 2016–2025 |
|---|---|---|---|---|---|---|---|---|---|---|---|---|---|
| Increase coal AML fee to pre-2006 levels | ...... | –49 | –50 | –51 | –52 | –52 | –52 | ...... | ...... | ...... | ...... | –254 | –306 |
| Strengthen Unemployment Insurance (UI) system solvency | ...... | ...... | –3,889 | –4,263 | –4,207 | –4,643 | –4,877 | –5,154 | –5,143 | –5,110 | –5,663 | –17,002 | –42,949 |
| Improve UI Extended Benefits | ...... | –50 | –191 | –195 | –251 | –343 | –416 | –457 | –423 | –435 | –455 | –1,030 | –3,216 |
| Modernize UI | ...... | ...... | ...... | –190 | –107 | –36 | –36 | ...... | ...... | ...... | ...... | –333 | –369 |
| Implement cap adjustments for UI program integrity | ...... | ...... | ...... | 4 | 15 | 19 | 28 | 43 | 46 | 54 | 64 | 39 | 274 |
| Improve UI program integrity (mandatory SIDES) | ...... | ...... | ...... | 1 | 2 | 2 | 4 | 6 | 8 | 9 | 10 | 5 | 42 |
| Allow use of prisoner database for UI program integrity | ...... | ...... | ...... | ...... | ...... | 2 | 2 | 2 | 3 | 4 | 5 | 2 | 18 |
| Implement tax enforcement program integrity cap adjustment | ...... | –432 | –1,451 | –2,926 | –4,476 | –6,095 | –7,481 | –8,475 | –9,077 | –9,503 | –9,819 | –15,380 | –59,735 |
| Reform inland waterways funding | ...... | –113 | –113 | –113 | –113 | –113 | –113 | –113 | –113 | –113 | –113 | –565 | –1,130 |
| Offset DI benefits for period of concurrent UI receipt | ...... | ...... | ...... | 1 | 2 | 6 | 15 | 18 | 22 | 27 | 36 | 8 | 126 |
| Enact immigration reform | ...... | –1,000 | –7,000 | –20,000 | –30,000 | –40,000 | –45,000 | –55,000 | –64,000 | –74,000 | –84,000 | –98,000 | –420,000 |
| Modernize military retirement | ...... | ...... | ...... | 122 | 176 | 185 | 200 | 219 | 236 | 257 | 273 | 483 | 1,668 |
| Total receipt effects of mandatory proposals | ...... | –1,848 | –13,134 | –28,225 | –40,148 | –52,189 | –58,320 | –69,516 | –79,059 | –89,442 | –100,309 | –135,544 | –532,191 |

[4] Health savings in S–2 includes all HHS health savings and OPM FEHBP savings.
[5] Unemployment insurance reform also includes the proposal to make the unemployment insurance surtax permanent. On net, the package reduces the deficit by $7.4 billion over 10 years.
[6] Revenues are net of the 20% Treasury offset.
[7] A version of this proposal was included in the Trade Preference Extension Act of 2015 (P.L. 114–27), which was enacted too late to be included in the Mid-Session Review estimates.
[8] Deficit savings achieved through the increased value of monetized spectrum achieved via targeted investments that will enhance Federal spectrum efficiency and create more opportunity for spectrum sharing.
[9] This proposal also saves less than $500,000 in SSI over 10 years.
[10] This proposal costs less than $500,000 in each year and over 5 and 10 years.
[11] Savings of $1 million over 5 years and $4 million over 10 years.
[12] The estimates for this proposal include effects on outlays. The outlay effects included in the totals above are as follows:

|  | 2015 | 2016 | 2017 | 2018 | 2019 | 2020 | 2021 | 2022 | 2023 | 2024 | 2025 | Totals 2016–2020 | Totals 2016–2025 |
|---|---|---|---|---|---|---|---|---|---|---|---|---|---|
| Reform child care tax incentives | ...... | 945 | 975 | 1,020 | 1,061 | 1,117 | 1,155 | 1,196 | 1,237 | 1,268 | 1,268 | 5,118 | 11,242 |
| Simplify and better target tax benefits for education | ...... | ...... | 1,852 | 4,804 | 4,784 | 4,826 | 5,140 | 5,448 | 5,511 | 5,936 | 6,095 | 16,266 | 44,396 |
| Provide for automatic enrollment in IRAs, including a small employer tax credit, increase the tax credit for small employer plan start-up costs, and provide an additional tax credit for small employer plans newly offering auto-enrollment | ...... | ...... | 129 | 199 | 201 | 209 | 210 | 215 | 219 | 228 | 232 | 738 | 1,842 |
| Expand EITC for workers without qualifying children | ...... | 275 | 5,495 | 5,506 | 5,538 | 5,619 | 5,722 | 5,822 | 5,930 | 6,031 | 6,131 | 22,433 | 52,069 |

## Table S-8. MANDATORY AND RECEIPT PROPOSALS—Continued
(Deficit increases (+) or decreases (−) in millions of dollars)

|  | 2015 | 2016 | 2017 | 2018 | 2019 | 2020 | 2021 | 2022 | 2023 | 2024 | 2025 | Totals 2016-2020 | Totals 2016-2025 |
|---|---|---|---|---|---|---|---|---|---|---|---|---|---|
| Simplify the rules for claiming the EITC for workers without qualifying children | ......... | 34 | 671 | 665 | 655 | 663 | 677 | 693 | 710 | 727 | 745 | 2,688 | 6,240 |
| Provide a second-earner tax credit | ......... | ......... | 739 | 737 | 747 | 754 | 762 | 770 | 770 | 777 | 777 | 2,977 | 6,833 |
| Designate Promise Zones | ......... | 13 | 27 | 28 | 29 | 31 | 32 | 34 | 35 | 37 | 38 | 128 | 304 |
| Provide the IRS with greater flexibility to address correctable errors | ......... | −25 | −53 | −55 | −55 | −57 | −58 | −58 | −59 | −61 | −62 | −245 | −543 |
| Rationalize tax return filing due dates so they are staggered | ......... | −21 | −22 | −23 | −23 | −24 | −24 | −24 | −25 | −25 | −26 | −113 | −237 |
| Explicitly provide that the Department of the Treasury and IRS have authority to regulate all paid return preparers | ......... | −3 | −14 | −16 | −17 | −20 | −21 | −23 | −24 | −26 | −28 | −70 | −192 |
| Total, outlay effects of receipt proposals | ......... | 1,218 | 9,799 | 12,865 | 12,920 | 13,118 | 13,595 | 14,073 | 14,304 | 14,892 | 15,170 | 49,920 | 121,954 |
| **Addendum, reserve for long-run revenue-neutral business tax reform:** | | | | | | | | | | | | | |
| Expand and simplify the tax credit provided to qualified small employers for non-elective contributions to employee health insurance | ......... | 22 | 35 | 31 | 22 | 19 | 11 | 11 | 6 | 6 | 4 | 129 | 167 |
| Modify and permanently extend renewable electricity production tax credit and investment tax credit | ......... | ......... | 19 | 46 | 61 | 73 | 86 | 105 | 132 | 160 | 187 | 199 | 869 |
| Provide a carbon dioxide investment and sequestration tax credit | ......... | ......... | ......... | ......... | 727 | 723 | 163 | 21 | 42 | 58 | 69 | 1,450 | 1,803 |
| Provide America Fast Forward Bonds and expand eligible uses | ......... | 306 | 1,397 | 3,006 | 4,689 | 6,438 | 8,244 | 10,101 | 11,994 | 13,911 | 15,845 | 15,836 | 75,931 |

[13] Revenues are net of the 25% Treasury offset.
[14] The effect of this proposal on receipts is shown above under tax proposals.
[15] This provision is estimated to have zero receipt effect under the Administration's current economic projections.

## Table S–9. FUNDING LEVELS FOR APPROPRIATED ("DISCRETIONARY") PROGRAMS BY CATEGORY

(Budget authority in billions of dollars)

| | Actual 2014 | Enacted 2015 | Request 2016 | 2017 | 2018 | 2019 | 2020 | Outyears 2021 | 2022 | 2023 | 2024 | 2025 | Totals 2016-2020 | 2016-2025 |
|---|---|---|---|---|---|---|---|---|---|---|---|---|---|---|
| **Discretionary Adjusted Baseline by Category:**[1] | | | | | | | | | | | | | | |
| Defense Category | 521 | 521 | 523 | 536 | 549 | 562 | 576 | 590 | 660 | 676 | 693 | 710 | 2,746 | 6,075 |
| Non-Defense Category | 514 | 508 | 493 | 504 | 516 | 530 | 543 | 556 | 604 | 619 | 635 | 650 | 2,587 | 5,652 |
| Total, Base Discretionary Funding | 1,035 | 1,029 | 1,017 | 1,040 | 1,065 | 1,092 | 1,119 | 1,146 | 1,264 | 1,295 | 1,327 | 1,360 | 5,334 | 11,727 |
| **Discretionary Policy Changes to Baseline Caps:**[2] | | | | | | | | | | | | | | |
| Proposed Cap Changes:[2] | | | | | | | | | | | | | | |
| Defense Category | | | +38 | +37 | +35 | +30 | +22 | +20 | –38 | –41 | –45 | –49 | +162 | +9 |
| Non-Defense Category | | | +37 | +37 | +35 | +30 | +22 | +20 | –16 | –18 | –21 | –23 | +160 | +101 |
| Non-Defense Category Reclassifications: | | | | | | | | | | | | | | |
| Surface Transportation Programs | –4 | –4 | –4 | –4 | –4 | –4 | –5 | –5 | –5 | –5 | –5 | –5 | –22 | –46 |
| Program Integrity | | | | –* | –* | –* | –* | –* | –* | –* | –* | –* | –1 | –2 |
| Contract Support Costs | | | | –1 | –1 | –1 | –1 | –1 | –1 | –1 | –1 | –1 | –4 | –10 |
| **Proposed Discretionary Policy by Category:** | | | | | | | | | | | | | | |
| Defense Category | 521 | 521 | 561 | 573 | 584 | 592 | 598 | 610 | 622 | 635 | 648 | 661 | 2,908 | 6,084 |
| Non-Defense Category | 510 | 504 | 526 | 535 | 545 | 554 | 559 | 570 | 582 | 595 | 608 | 620 | 2,720 | 5,694 |
| Total, Base Discretionary Funding | 1,031 | 1,025 | 1,087 | 1,108 | 1,129 | 1,146 | 1,157 | 1,180 | 1,204 | 1,230 | 1,256 | 1,281 | 5,628 | 11,778 |
| **Discretionary Cap Adjustments and Other Funding (not included above):**[3] | | | | | | | | | | | | | | |
| Overseas Contingency Operations[4] | 92 | 74 | 58 | 27 | 27 | 27 | 27 | 27 | | | | | 165 | 191 |
| Disaster Relief | 6 | 7 | 7 | | | | | | | | | | 7 | 7 |
| Program Integrity | 1 | 1 | 2 | 1 | 2 | 2 | 3 | 3 | 3 | 3 | 3 | 3 | 11 | 25 |
| Wildfire Suppression | | | 1 | 1 | 1 | 1 | 1 | 1 | 1 | 1 | 1 | 1 | 5 | 11 |
| Other Emergency/Supplemental Funding | * | 5 | | | | | | | | | | | | |
| Total, Cap Adjustments and Other | 99 | 87 | 68 | 29 | 30 | 30 | 30 | 31 | 4 | 4 | 4 | 4 | 188 | 235 |
| **Grand Total, Discretionary Budget Authority** | 1,129 | 1,112 | 1,155 | 1,138 | 1,159 | 1,176 | 1,188 | 1,211 | 1,208 | 1,234 | 1,260 | 1,286 | 5,815 | 12,013 |

# Table S–9. FUNDING LEVELS FOR APPROPRIATED ("DISCRETIONARY") PROGRAMS BY CATEGORY—Continued

(Budget authority in billions of dollars)

*Memorandum: Current Law and Proposed Changes to Existing BBEDCA Caps [5]*

|  | 2016 | 2017 | 2018 | 2019 | 2020 | 2021 | 2016-2021 |
|---|---|---|---|---|---|---|---|
| Joint Committee Reductions | –90 | –91 | –91 | –90 | –89 | –88 | –538 |
| 2016 Budget Proposed Addback to caps | +74 | +74 | +70 | +60 | +44 | +40 | +361 |

\* Less than $500 million.

[1] The discretionary funding levels from OMB's adjusted baseline are consistent with the caps in the Balanced Budget and Emergency Deficit Control Act (BBEDCA) with separate categories of funding for "defense" (or Function 050) and "non-defense" for 2015-2021. These baseline levels assume Joint Committee enforcement cap reductions are in effect through 2021. For 2022 through 2025, programs are assumed to grow at current services growth rates with Joint Committee enforcement no longer in effect, consistent with current law. The levels shown here for the non-defense category do not include the reclassification of surface transportation programs shown later in the table.

[2] The 2016 Budget provides a detailed request for 2016 at the cap levels requested in the 2015 Budget and, after 2016, continues the 2015 Budget framework of providing additional investments in both defense and non-defense programs above the baseline levels that include Joint Committee enforcement.

[3] Where applicable, amounts in 2014 through 2025 are existing or proposed cap adjustments designated pursuant to Section 251(b)(2) of BBEDCA. The 2016 Budget proposes new cap adjustments for program integrity and wildfire suppression activities. For 2017 through 2025, the cap adjustment levels for wildfire suppression are a placeholder that increase at the policy growth rates in the President's Budget. The existing disaster relief cap adjustment ceiling (which is determined one year at a time) would be reduced by the amount provided for wildfire suppression activities under the cap adjustment for the preceding fiscal year. The amounts will be refined in subsequent Budgets as data on the average costs for wildfire suppression activities are updated annually.

[4] The 2016 Budget includes placeholder amounts of nearly $27 billion per year for Government-wide OCO funding from 2017 to 2021. The placeholder amounts continue to reflect a total OCO budget authority cap from 2013 to 2021 of $450 billion, in line with previous years' policy, but do not reflect any specific decisions or assumptions about OCO funding in any particular year. These amounts do not reflect the Administration's intent to transition all enduring costs currently funded in the OCO budget to the base budget beginning in FY 2017 and ending by FY 2020. Those amounts will be refined in subsequent Budgets as the Administration develops its OCO transition plan.

[5] Under Joint Committee enforcement, the current law defense and non-defense discretionary caps specified in BBEDCA are estimated to be reduced by a combined $538 billion over the 2016 through 2021 period. The 2016 Budget proposes to restore approximately two-thirds of those reductions.

## Table S–10. FUNDING LEVELS FOR APPROPRIATED ("DISCRETIONARY") PROGRAMS BY AGENCY

(Budget authority in billions of dollars)

| | Actual 2014 | Enacted 2015 | Request 2016 | 2017 | 2018 | 2019 | 2020 | 2021 | 2022 | 2023 | 2024 | 2025 | Totals 2016-2020 | Totals 2016-2025 |
|---|---|---|---|---|---|---|---|---|---|---|---|---|---|---|
| **Base Discretionary Funding by Agency:**[1] | | | | | | | | | | | | | | |
| Agriculture | 24.3 | 24.2 | 23.5 | 25.2 | 25.5 | 25.7 | 26.0 | 26.5 | 27.1 | 27.6 | 28.2 | 28.7 | 125.9 | 264.0 |
| Commerce | 8.3 | 8.6 | 9.8 | 10.3 | 10.7 | 11.9 | 15.5 | 10.6 | 10.4 | 10.7 | 10.8 | 11.3 | 58.3 | 112.1 |
| *Census Bureau* | *0.9* | *1.1* | *1.5* | *1.8* | *2.1* | *3.2* | *6.7* | *1.6* | *1.2* | *1.3* | *1.3* | *1.5* | *15.2* | *22.1* |
| Defense[2] | 496.0 | 496.1 | 534.3 | 547.3 | 556.4 | 564.4 | 570.0 | 581.4 | 593.0 | 604.9 | 617.0 | 629.3 | 2,772.4 | 5,798.1 |
| Education | 67.3 | 67.1 | 70.7 | 71.7 | 72.7 | 73.2 | 73.7 | 74.7 | 75.8 | 76.8 | 77.9 | 79.0 | 362.0 | 746.3 |
| Energy | 27.2 | 27.3 | 29.9 | 29.3 | 30.0 | 30.7 | 31.0 | 31.6 | 32.3 | 32.9 | 33.6 | 34.3 | 151.0 | 315.7 |
| *National Nuclear Security Administration*[2] | *11.2* | *11.4* | *12.6* | *11.5* | *11.7* | *12.2* | *12.3* | *12.6* | *12.8* | *13.1* | *13.3* | *13.6* | *60.3* | *125.7* |
| Health & Human Services[3] | 79.8 | 80.2 | 79.9 | 86.3 | 88.0 | 88.8 | 89.7 | 91.5 | 93.3 | 95.2 | 97.1 | 99.0 | 432.6 | 908.9 |
| Homeland Security | 39.8 | 39.8 | 41.2 | 41.6 | 42.2 | 42.5 | 42.9 | 43.8 | 44.8 | 45.7 | 45.0 | 45.9 | 210.4 | 435.6 |
| Housing and Urban Development | 34.2 | 31.6 | 41.1 | 41.8 | 42.6 | 43.0 | 43.4 | 44.2 | 45.0 | 45.8 | 46.7 | 47.5 | 211.9 | 441.1 |
| Interior | 11.7 | 12.1 | 12.9 | 12.9 | 13.1 | 13.3 | 13.4 | 13.7 | 14.0 | 14.2 | 14.5 | 14.8 | 65.6 | 136.8 |
| Justice | 27.3 | 26.2 | 14.9 | 29.4 | 30.0 | 30.3 | 30.6 | 31.2 | 31.9 | 32.5 | 33.1 | 33.8 | 135.3 | 297.8 |
| Labor | 12.0 | 11.9 | 13.2 | 13.4 | 13.6 | 13.7 | 13.8 | 14.1 | 14.3 | 14.6 | 14.8 | 15.1 | 67.7 | 140.6 |
| State and Other International Programs | 42.9 | 40.1 | 46.3 | 47.2 | 48.1 | 48.6 | 48.9 | 49.9 | 50.9 | 51.9 | 52.9 | 54.0 | 239.0 | 498.5 |
| Transportation | 13.6 | 13.8 | 14.4 | 14.6 | 14.9 | 15.1 | 15.2 | 15.5 | 15.8 | 16.2 | 16.5 | 16.8 | 74.2 | 155.1 |
| Treasury | 12.7 | 12.3 | 12.8 | 14.0 | 14.3 | 14.5 | 14.8 | 15.1 | 15.5 | 15.8 | 16.2 | 16.5 | 70.4 | 149.5 |
| Veterans Affairs | 63.3 | 65.1 | 70.2 | 75.1 | 76.7 | 78.3 | 79.9 | 81.6 | 83.5 | 85.6 | 87.6 | 89.7 | 380.1 | 808.1 |
| Corps of Engineers | 5.7 | 5.5 | 4.7 | 4.8 | 4.9 | 5.0 | 5.0 | 5.1 | 5.2 | 5.3 | 5.4 | 5.5 | 24.5 | 51.1 |
| Environmental Protection Agency | 8.2 | 8.1 | 8.6 | 8.8 | 8.9 | 9.0 | 9.1 | 9.3 | 9.5 | 9.7 | 9.9 | 10.1 | 44.4 | 92.8 |
| General Services Administration | 2.0 | –0.4 | 0.8 | 0.3 | 0.3 | 0.3 | 0.3 | 0.3 | 0.3 | 0.3 | 0.3 | 0.3 | 1.9 | 3.4 |
| National Aeronautics & Space Administration | 17.6 | 18.0 | 18.5 | 18.9 | 19.3 | 19.5 | 19.7 | 20.1 | 20.5 | 20.9 | 21.3 | 21.7 | 95.8 | 200.2 |
| National Science Foundation | 7.2 | 7.3 | 7.7 | 7.9 | 8.0 | 8.1 | 8.2 | 8.4 | 8.5 | 8.7 | 8.9 | 9.1 | 39.9 | 83.5 |
| Small Business Administration | 0.9 | 0.9 | 0.7 | 0.7 | 0.7 | 0.7 | 0.7 | 0.8 | 0.8 | 0.8 | 0.8 | 0.8 | 3.6 | 7.6 |
| Social Security Administration[3] | 8.9 | 9.0 | 9.6 | 9.4 | 9.6 | 9.7 | 9.8 | 10.0 | 10.2 | 10.4 | 10.6 | 10.8 | 48.1 | 100.1 |
| Corporation for National & Community Service | 1.0 | 1.1 | 1.2 | 1.2 | 1.2 | 1.2 | 1.3 | 1.3 | 1.3 | 1.3 | 1.4 | 1.4 | 6.1 | 12.8 |
| Other Agencies | 18.8 | 19.0 | 20.0 | 20.0 | 20.4 | 20.7 | 20.8 | 21.2 | 21.6 | 22.1 | 22.5 | 22.9 | 101.9 | 212.2 |
| Allowances[4] | ........ | ........ | –0.1 | –23.5 | –23.0 | –22.1 | –26.9 | –22.0 | –21.6 | –20.0 | –17.3 | –17.0 | –95.5 | –193.4 |
| **Subtotal, Base Discretionary Funding** | **1,030.8** | **1,024.9** | **1,086.8** | **1,108.4** | **1,129.3** | **1,146.2** | **1,157.1** | **1,180.0** | **1,203.8** | **1,229.7** | **1,255.6** | **1,281.5** | **5,627.7** | **11,778.3** |
| **Discretionary Cap Adjustments and Other Funding (not included above):**[5] | | | | | | | | | | | | | | |
| Overseas Contingency Operations | 91.9 | 73.7 | 58.0 | 26.7 | 26.7 | 26.7 | 26.7 | 26.7 | ........ | ........ | ........ | ........ | 164.7 | 191.3 |
| Defense | 85.2 | 64.2 | 50.9 | ........ | ........ | ........ | ........ | ........ | ........ | ........ | ........ | ........ | 50.9 | 50.9 |

# SUMMARY TABLES

## Table S–10. FUNDING LEVELS FOR APPROPRIATED ("DISCRETIONARY") PROGRAMS BY AGENCY—Continued

(Budget authority in billions of dollars)

| | Actual 2014 | Enacted 2015 | Request 2016 | Outyears 2017 | 2018 | 2019 | 2020 | 2021 | 2022 | 2023 | 2024 | 2025 | Totals 2016-2020 | 2016-2025 |
|---|---|---|---|---|---|---|---|---|---|---|---|---|---|---|
| Homeland Security | 0.2 | 0.2 | | | | | | | | | | | | |
| State and Other International Programs | 6.5 | 9.3 | 7.0 | | | | | | | | | | 7.0 | 7.0 |
| Overseas Contingency Operations Outyears[6] | | | | 26.7 | 26.7 | 26.7 | 26.7 | 26.7 | | | | | 106.7 | 133.3 |
| **Program Integrity** | **0.9** | **1.5** | **2.3** | **1.5** | **1.9** | **2.3** | **2.7** | **2.8** | **2.8** | **2.9** | **3.0** | **3.1** | **10.6** | **25.1** |
| Health & Human Services | | 0.4 | 0.4 | 0.4 | 0.4 | 0.5 | 0.5 | 0.5 | 0.5 | 0.5 | 0.6 | 0.6 | 2.2 | 4.9 |
| Labor | | | * | * | * | * | * | 0.1 | 0.1 | 0.1 | 0.1 | 0.1 | 0.2 | 0.5 |
| Treasury | | | 0.7 | 1.0 | 1.4 | 1.8 | 2.2 | 2.2 | 2.3 | 2.3 | 2.4 | 2.4 | 7.0 | 18.6 |
| SSA | 0.9 | 1.1 | 1.2 | | | | | | | | | | 1.2 | 1.2 |
| **Disaster Relief** | **5.6** | **6.5** | **6.9** | | | | | | | | | | **6.9** | **6.9** |
| Agriculture | | 0.1 | | | | | | | | | | | | |
| Homeland Security | 5.6 | 6.4 | 6.7 | | | | | | | | | | 6.7 | 6.7 |
| Small Business Administration | | | 0.2 | | | | | | | | | | 0.2 | 0.2 |
| **Wildfire Suppression**[7] | | | **1.1** | **1.1** | **1.1** | **1.1** | **1.1** | **1.1** | **1.2** | **1.2** | **1.2** | **1.2** | **5.5** | **11.4** |
| Agriculture | | | 0.9 | 0.9 | 0.9 | 0.9 | 0.9 | 0.9 | 0.9 | 1.0 | 1.0 | 1.0 | 4.4 | 9.2 |
| Interior | | | 0.2 | 0.2 | 0.2 | 0.2 | 0.2 | 0.2 | 0.2 | 0.2 | 0.2 | 0.2 | 1.0 | 2.2 |
| **Other Emergency Funding** | **0.2** | **5.4** | | | | | | | | | | | | |
| Defense | 0.2 | 0.1 | | | | | | | | | | | | |
| Health & Human Services | | 2.8 | | | | | | | | | | | | |
| State and Other International Programs | | 2.5 | | | | | | | | | | | | |
| **Grand Total, Discretionary Funding** | **1,129.5** | **1,112.0** | **1,154.9** | **1,137.6** | **1,158.9** | **1,176.2** | **1,187.0** | **1,210.5** | **1,233.8** | **1,259.8** | **1,285.8** | **5,815.3** | **12,013.0** |

* $50 million or less.

[1] Amounts in the actual and enacted years of 2014 and 2015 exclude changes in mandatory programs enacted in appropriations bills since those amounts have been rebased as mandatory, whereas amounts in 2016 are net of these proposals.

[2] The Department of Defense (DOD) levels in 2017–2025 include funding that will be allocated, in annual increments, to the National Nuclear Security Administration (NNSA). Current estimates by which DOD's budget authority will decrease and NNSA's will increase are, in millions of dollars: 2017: $1,602; 2018: $1,665; 2019: $1,693; 2020: $1,735; 2017–2025: $15,910. DOD and NNSA are reviewing NNSA's outyear requirements and these will be included in future reports to the Congress.

[3] Funding from the Hospital Insurance and Supplementary Medical Insurance trust funds for administrative expenses incurred by the Social Security Administration that support the Medicare program are included in the Health and Human Services total and not in the Social Security Administration total.

[4] The 2016 Budget includes allowances, similar to the Function 920 allowances used in Budget Resolutions, to represent amounts to be allocated among the respective agencies to reach the proposed defense and non-defense caps for 2017 and beyond. These levels are determined for illustrative purposes but do not reflect specific policy decisions.

[5] Where applicable, amounts in 2014 through 2025 are existing or proposed cap adjustments designated pursuant to Section 251(b)(2) of BBEDCA.

[6] The 2016 Budget includes placeholder amounts of nearly $27 billion per year for Government-wide OCO funding from 2017 to 2021. The placeholder amounts continue to reflect a total OCO budget authority cap from 2013 to 2021 of $450 billion, in line with previous years' policy, but do not reflect any specific decisions or assumptions about OCO funding in any particular year. These amounts do not reflect the Administration's intent to transition all enduring costs currently funded in the OCO budget to the base budget beginning in 2017 and ending by 2020. Those amounts will be refined in subsequent Budgets as the Administration develops its OCO transition plan.

[7] For 2017 through 2025, the cap adjustment levels are a placeholder that increase at the policy growth rates in the President's Budget. The existing disaster relief cap adjustment ceiling (which is determined one year at a time) would be reduced by the amount provided for wildfire suppression activities under the cap adjustment for the preceding fiscal year. Those amounts will be refined in subsequent Budgets as data on the average costs for wildfire suppression are updated annually.

## Table S–11. FEDERAL GOVERNMENT FINANCING AND DEBT
(Dollar amounts in billions)

| | Actual 2014 | 2015 | 2016 | 2017 | 2018 | 2019 | 2020 | 2021 | 2022 | 2023 | 2024 | 2025 |
|---|---|---|---|---|---|---|---|---|---|---|---|---|
| **Financing:** | | | | | | | | | | | | |
| **Unified budget deficit:** | | | | | | | | | | | | |
| Primary deficit (+)/surplus (–) | 256 | 244 | 180 | 132 | 116 | 100 | 60 | 56 | 27 | 2 | –22 | –19 |
| Net interest | 229 | 210 | 250 | 305 | 365 | 434 | 503 | 561 | 616 | 670 | 716 | 761 |
| Unified budget deficit | 485 | 455 | 429 | 436 | 481 | 533 | 563 | 617 | 643 | 672 | 695 | 742 |
| As a percent of GDP | 2.8% | 2.6% | 2.3% | 2.2% | 2.4% | 2.5% | 2.5% | 2.7% | 2.7% | 2.7% | 2.7% | 2.7% |
| **Other transactions affecting borrowing from the public:** | | | | | | | | | | | | |
| Changes in financial assets and liabilities:[1] | | | | | | | | | | | | |
| Change in Treasury operating cash balance | 70 | 42 | ...... | ...... | ...... | ...... | ...... | ...... | ...... | ...... | ...... | ...... |
| Net disbursements of credit financing accounts: | | | | | | | | | | | | |
| Direct loan accounts | 121 | 125 | 138 | 135 | 131 | 127 | 122 | 117 | 115 | 118 | 116 | 116 |
| Guaranteed loan accounts | 12 | 11 | –3 | –3 | –1 | –2 | –4 | –4 | –5 | –8 | –8 | –9 |
| Troubled Asset Relief Program (TARP) equity purchase accounts | –6 | –1 | –* | –* | –* | –* | –* | –* | –* | –* | –* | –* |
| Net purchases of non-Federal securities by the National Railroad Retirement Investment Trust (NRRIT) | 1 | * | –1 | –1 | –1 | –1 | –1 | –1 | –1 | –* | –* | –* |
| Net change in other financial assets and liabilities[2] | 114 | ...... | ...... | ...... | ...... | ...... | ...... | ...... | ...... | ...... | ...... | ...... |
| Subtotal, changes in financial assets and liabilities | 313 | 177 | 134 | 131 | 130 | 125 | 120 | 112 | 109 | 110 | 108 | 107 |
| Seigniorage on coins | –* | –* | –* | –* | –* | –* | –* | –* | –* | –* | –* | –* |
| Total, other transactions affecting borrowing from the public | 313 | 177 | 134 | 131 | 129 | 125 | 120 | 112 | 108 | 109 | 107 | 106 |
| Total, requirement to borrow from the public (equals change in debt held by the public) | 797 | 631 | 563 | 567 | 611 | 658 | 682 | 729 | 752 | 781 | 802 | 848 |
| **Changes in Debt Subject to Statutory Limitation:** | | | | | | | | | | | | |
| Change in debt held by the public | 797 | 631 | 563 | 567 | 611 | 658 | 682 | 729 | 752 | 781 | 802 | 848 |
| Change in debt held by Government accounts | 278 | 115 | 132 | 175 | 169 | 130 | 96 | 81 | –9 | –17 | –3 | –65 |
| Change in other factors | 7 | 1 | 2 | 2 | 2 | 3 | 2 | 2 | 2 | 2 | 1 | * |
| Total, change in debt subject to statutory limitation | 1,082 | 746 | 697 | 744 | 782 | 791 | 781 | 812 | 744 | 765 | 801 | 783 |
| **Debt Subject to Statutory Limitation, End of Year:** | | | | | | | | | | | | |
| Debt issued by Treasury | 17,768 | 18,513 | 19,208 | 19,951 | 20,732 | 21,522 | 22,301 | 23,112 | 23,854 | 24,619 | 25,419 | 26,202 |
| Adjustment for discount, premium, and coverage[3] | 13 | 15 | 17 | 18 | 19 | 21 | 22 | 24 | 25 | 26 | 27 | 27 |
| Total, debt subject to statutory limitation[4] | 17,781 | 18,528 | 19,225 | 19,969 | 20,751 | 21,542 | 22,323 | 23,135 | 23,879 | 24,645 | 25,446 | 26,229 |
| **Debt Outstanding, End of Year:** | | | | | | | | | | | | |
| Gross Federal debt:[5] | | | | | | | | | | | | |
| Debt issued by Treasury | 17,768 | 18,513 | 19,208 | 19,951 | 20,732 | 21,522 | 22,301 | 23,112 | 23,854 | 24,619 | 25,419 | 26,202 |
| Debt issued by other agencies | 26 | 27 | 27 | 27 | 25 | 24 | 23 | 22 | 22 | 22 | 21 | 21 |
| Total, gross Federal debt | 17,794 | 18,540 | 19,235 | 19,978 | 20,757 | 21,546 | 22,324 | 23,134 | 23,877 | 24,640 | 25,440 | 26,222 |

## Table S-11. FEDERAL GOVERNMENT FINANCING AND DEBT—Continued
(Dollar amounts in billions)

| | Actual 2014 | 2015 | 2016 | 2017 | 2018 | 2019 | 2020 | 2021 | 2022 | 2023 | 2024 | 2025 |
|---|---|---|---|---|---|---|---|---|---|---|---|---|
| **Held by:** | | | | | | | | | | | | |
| Debt held by Government accounts | 5,015 | 5,129 | 5,261 | 5,436 | 5,605 | 5,735 | 5,832 | 5,913 | 5,903 | 5,886 | 5,883 | 5,818 |
| Debt held by the public⁶ | 12,780 | 13,411 | 13,974 | 14,541 | 15,152 | 15,810 | 16,493 | 17,221 | 17,973 | 18,754 | 19,556 | 20,404 |
| As a percent of GDP | 74.0% | 75.3% | 75.3% | 74.9% | 74.6% | 74.6% | 74.6% | 74.6% | 74.6% | 74.6% | 74.6% | 74.6% |
| **Debt Held by the Public Net of Financial Assets:** | | | | | | | | | | | | |
| Debt held by the public | 12,780 | 13,411 | 13,974 | 14,541 | 15,152 | 15,810 | 16,493 | 17,221 | 17,973 | 18,754 | 19,556 | 20,404 |
| Less financial assets net of liabilities: | | | | | | | | | | | | |
| Treasury operating cash balance | 158 | 200 | 200 | 200 | 200 | 200 | 200 | 200 | 200 | 200 | 200 | 200 |
| Credit financing account balances: | | | | | | | | | | | | |
| Direct loan accounts | 1,065 | 1,190 | 1,327 | 1,462 | 1,593 | 1,721 | 1,843 | 1,960 | 2,075 | 2,193 | 2,309 | 2,425 |
| Guaranteed loan accounts | 2 | 13 | 10 | 8 | 7 | 6 | 4 | –6 | –6 | –13 | –22 | –30 |
| TARP equity purchase accounts | 1 | * | * | * | * | * | * | * | * | * | –1 | –1 |
| Government-sponsored enterprise preferred stock | 96 | 96 | 96 | 96 | 96 | 96 | 96 | 96 | 96 | 96 | 96 | 96 |
| Non-Federal securities held by NRRIT | 25 | 25 | 25 | 24 | 23 | 23 | 22 | 22 | 21 | 21 | 21 | 21 |
| Other assets net of liabilities | –23 | –23 | –23 | –23 | –23 | –23 | –23 | –23 | –23 | –23 | –23 | –23 |
| Total, financial assets net of liabilities | 1,324 | 1,501 | 1,636 | 1,767 | 1,897 | 2,022 | 2,142 | 2,254 | 2,363 | 2,473 | 2,580 | 2,687 |
| Debt held by the public net of financial assets | 11,455 | 11,910 | 12,339 | 12,775 | 13,256 | 13,789 | 14,351 | 14,967 | 15,610 | 16,281 | 16,976 | 17,717 |
| As a percent of GDP | 66.4% | 66.9% | 66.5% | 65.8% | 65.3% | 65.1% | 64.9% | 64.9% | 64.8% | 64.8% | 64.8% | 64.8% |

* $500 million or less.

¹ A decrease in the Treasury operating cash balance (which is an asset) is a means of financing a deficit and therefore has a negative sign; that is, the reduction in cash balances reduces the amount that would otherwise be borrowed from the public. An increase in checks outstanding (which is a liability) is also a means of financing a deficit and therefore also has a negative sign.

² Includes checks outstanding, accrued interest payable on Treasury debt, uninvested deposit fund balances, allocations of special drawing rights, and other liability accounts; and, as an offset, cash and monetary assets (other than the Treasury operating cash balance), other asset accounts, and profit on sale of gold.

³ Consists mainly of debt issued by the Federal Financing Bank (which is not subject to limit), Treasury securities held by the Federal Financing Bank, the unamortized discount (less premium) on public issues of Treasury notes and bonds (other than zero-coupon bonds), and the unrealized discount on Government account series securities.

⁴ Legislation enacted February 15, 2014, suspended the debt limit through March 15, 2015. In accordance with that legislation (P.L. 113-83), the debt limit was increased to $18,113 billion effective March 16, 2015.

⁵ Treasury securities held by the public and zero-coupon bonds held by Government accounts are almost all measured at sales price plus amortized discount or less amortized premium. Agency debt securities are almost all measured at face value. Treasury securities in the Government account series are otherwise measured at face value less unrealized discount (if any).

⁶ At the end of 2014, the Federal Reserve Banks held $2,451.7 billion of Federal securities and the rest of the public held $10,328.1 billion. Debt held by the Federal Reserve Banks is not estimated for future years.

www.ingramcontent.com/pod-product-compliance
Lightning Source LLC
Chambersburg PA
CBHW080724190526
45169CB00006B/2512